Positive Puppy Training 101

The Ultimate Practical Guide to Raising an Amazing and Happy Dog Without Causing Your Dog Stress or Harm With Modern Training Methods

Table of Contents

Introduction _____ 4

Going Positive _____ 6

   The Benefits _____ 8

   The Rewards _____ 12

Home Sweet Home _____ 17

   Shopping for the Essentials _____ 17

   Puppy-Proofing Your House _____ 24

   Getting Introduced _____ 29

The Food Dilemma _____ 35

House Training Your Puppy _____ 40

   Getting Used to the Crate _____ 41

   Learning to Accept the Leash _____ 49

   Potty Training _____ 58

Training Through Puppy's Growth Stages _ 70

   8 to 12 Weeks _____ 71

   12 to 16 Weeks _____ 79

   16 to 24 Weeks _____ 104

   6 to 9 Months _____ 123

   9 to 12 Months _____ 130

Giving the Clicker a Try _____ 133
Correcting Behavior Problems _____ 139
   Shushing the Barker _____ 139
   Not Accepting Biting _____ 144
   Getting Chewing Under Control _____ 146
   Stopping the Digging Frenzy _____ 148
   Discouraging the Jumper _____ 151
Dealing with Separation Anxiety _____ 153
Conclusion _____ 157

Introduction

Whether you are thinking about adopting a puppy or you have already added a cuddly member to your family, only to witness the exciting and cheerful moment being overshadowed by the chaos of disobedience, you are definitely in the right place. This book offers you all of the necessary tools required for instilling order from the minute you bring your bundle of joy home throughout its first year.

It doesn't matter which type of breed you own – all puppies can be trained. There is no such thing as a disobedient puppy, only an uncommitted owner. The purpose of this book is to show you, the dog owner, how to be the best trainer you can be, and help your puppy grow into a healthy, obedient, and happy dog.

The training success depends on how effective your communication is and just how committed you are to do the training drills on a daily basis. But, training your puppy shouldn't be a task you can hardly get through. It should be a fun and enjoyable time for both of you that will result in a strong and positive dog-owner relationship.

Revealing to you the secrets of positive reinforcement and teaching you how to approach your training process with the puppy's growth stages in mind, this book contains everything you need in order to instill proper discipline during the first and trickiest year of your dog's life. From how to prepare your house for your puppy, teach him that his teeth are not for your new shoes, to training him to become a respectful and obedient dog, this guide will show you that training your puppy is something that you will look forward to.

Now, grab some doggy treats and jump to the first chapter to learn all about training with love.

Going Positive

If the cuddly addition to your family is not your first interaction with dogs, then you are probably well aware that getting your dog to resist the urge to chew on your new sofa is not an easy task. It requires time, love, commitment, and most importantly patience. But luckily for the dog owners, puppies are just like babies. They are incredibly adaptive creatures that can soak your commands in like sponges. But the way in which you tell your puppy to sit or stop barking is of crucial importance, not only for the success of the training process but for the strength of your relationship with the dog, as well.

If you are thinking about taking the heavy-handed approach just because that's how dogs were trained in your time, you are making a huge mistake. In order for you to form a loving relationship with your puppy and help him grow into an obedient dog, you need to step away from the traditional methods.

Traditional training methods involve a leash that is used to correct the dog's behavior, such as pulling on the training leash when walking. But besides being cruel, traditional puppy training is also inefficient in most cases because the dog ends up feeling the strength of the leash often too late, and the training process becomes a painful and confusing process for the puppy. Not to mention that you cannot traditionally train a young puppy as all that pulling can end up causing neck injuries.

Choosing to go positive, on the other hand, is the best way to ensure that your puppy will be trained the right way while feeling loved at the same time. **Positive reinforcement** uses non-confrontational training methods in order to work your puppy's brain – by giving them rewards for positive behavior.

This training method has become extremely popular in the last decade as it has been promoted by some of the best dog trainers (such as Dawn Sylvia-Stasiewicz who used this method to train Bo, the Obama's dog).

The concept behind positive reinforcement training is pretty simple – by rewarding the good behavior you increase the chances of it being repeated. And the best part? This training method can be started the day you bring your pup home – any puppy can handle getting treats and being praised. Just keep in mind that the only way this training can work is if you reward the desired behavior immediately after it happens. That way your puppy can associate the reward with that behavior and become encouraged to repeat it again in the future. Obviously, the more you praise, the better your pup will learn what behavior gives him the treats and what doesn't.

The Benefits

Positive reinforcement is the only training method that is suitable for young puppies and therefore, very appealing to dog owners. It allows you to establish ground rules and proper behavior in a pretty short amount of time. And time is usually what dog owners are concerned with the most when deciding on how to train their puppies, once you begin this journey, you will soon realize that being a fast and effective training method is actually not the best thing about positive reinforcement. It is actually the fact that it's a fun process that boosts the confidence and enthusiasm in your puppy and you as its owner.

Besides being the most humane way to teach obedience, choosing to train your puppy with praising and rewards will throw many other benefits your way:

Training for Everyone

Unlike other training methods that put only one person in charge in order to show dominance that the puppy should obey, positive reinforcement allows everyone in the family to become a part of the training process. This method can never result in danger. For instance, unlike the traditional training where a child pulling on a leash or using another correction method can hurt the puppy (or in some cases even the child), teaching your child the commands you are using and filling their pockets with doggy treats can be nothing but fun.

Communication Establishment

Positive reinforcement is the only way in which you can establish solid communication with your puppy. You use a command to tell your puppy what to do, and then give rewards when the desired action is completed. When you start praising after every good behavior, your dog will be motivated and encouraged to repeat those actions as it is in their nature to please. This will allow you to communicate with the puppy in a clear way.

Punishing in order to correct behavior and teach a new one is not always so clear. Imagine your puppy has urinated on your new carpet. You use the old trick by smacking it with a rolled-up newspaper with the purpose of teaching that urinating on carpets is off limits. But, the chances of your puppy misinterpreting your intention are pretty high. For instance, your puppy could associate the punishment with not being allowed to urinate in your presence, which is why many dog owners who use traditional training never seem to catch their puppies and older dogs in the act of making a mess. Instead, the dogs have accidents when alone. That is clearly a problem in communication as fear is not an effective way to instill order.

Using rewards to praise, on the other hand, will result in no confusion. Your puppy will clearly detect why it is being rewarded, which will encourage it to repeat the desired behavior.

Perfect for All Breeds

Besides being cruel, traditional training methods like leash correction and other forms of punishments are not that effective, simply because they are not suitable for every breed type. Some dog types that are aggressive in nature can become even more aggressive when faced with punishments. On the other hand, fearful dogs can become even more fearful and may not respond well to even the smallest form of behavioral correction.

Trainers who use positive reinforcement have reported effectiveness and success in training all breeds, aggressive and fearful dogs included. This training method can be used for a variety of behaviors, so no matter what type of puppy you are thinking about adopting, positive reinforcement can definitely help you establish good communication and teach proper habits.

Bond Strengthening

If you are thinking about getting a puppy or have already adopted one, then chances are, you want it to become a part of your family and to be your companion and friend. Choosing to teach obedience with positive reinforcement is the perfect way to strengthen the dog-owner relationship. The difference between this training method and the outdated, traditional ones, is that positive reinforcement helps you not only to teach your puppy how to behave, but it also allows you to establish trust and strengthen the bond between the two of you.

Try to look at things from the puppy's perspective. Would you be more comfortable to work in a firm where the boss rewards you for finishing important projects or where you are physically forced and pushed to get things done? Your puppy is more likely to enjoy spending time with you if your communication is positive and if you praise the proper behavior.

Mental Stimulation

The most common behavioral problems arise out of boredom. If your puppy's day is not fulfilled and is left to sit around the house or backyard all day, it will try to tell you that in the form of digging, scratching, or chewing. By having a couple of positive training sessions each day, your puppy will burn enough energy to keep it content and not get bored.

It's Fun!

If your training is positive, upbeat, and short, it may turn out to be a lot of fun, not only for your puppy but for you too. By praising and rewarding, your puppy will quickly realize that good behavior leads to its favorite treats and therefore will try to repeat those actions in the hopes of being rewarded. Shortly after starting the positive reinforcement training, your puppy will look at the sessions as playtime, so teaching him new commands will be a breeze for you both.

The Rewards

The core of positive reinforcement is the reward. In order to reinforce a behavior that you like, you give your puppy a reward for the performed action to encourage it to associate the action with the reward, learn the behavioral pattern that gives it the treat and repeat it again in the future.

Those who choose other training methods usually step away from positive reinforcement because they look at the rewards as bribes. Like luring a three-year-old with chocolate to get them to listen to you, day after day. But bribing and rewarding are very different things. Think of your paycheck for a second. Does your boss bribe you with money to get you to work and contribute to the firm? No – you are rewarded for your hard work at the end of each month. If you stop getting paid for your work, you will not only decrease your performance but will actually stop coming to work. The same thing goes for your puppy. If it doesn't have a stimulus that will encourage it to behave in a certain way, it will not bother to complete the desired action. It's as simple as that.

But, even though the first thing that comes to mind when thinking about rewarding a puppy is small bone-shaped doggy treats, there are many different ways in which you can reward your dog's good behavior. Each dog is different and not all puppies respond the same to things. Knowing what your puppy is like and finding out what motivates it can help you train your pooch with success and have tons of fun along the way.

Treats

Treats are the most common reward for a reason. They are easy to dispense and perfect for giving an immediate reward. Besides, food is what most pups are interested in the most, so that's a pretty good reason to fill your pockets with tiny doggy treats when heading to the park. When trying to successfully train a puppy in a short amount of time, rewarding them with doggy treats is the best choice.

So, why someone would choose another reward, you may wonder. Besides the fact that some people find carrying treats around to be inconvenient, many pups who have digestive issues, weight problems, or are struggling with food allergies, should be rewarded another way.

Games

Just like treats, puppies love playing games. Spend some time with your pup trying out different games and see what it enjoys the most. Give your pooch a command in order for it to perform an action, and as soon as it does it, initiate its favorite game. That could be anything that the two of you have fun doing, or you can play it safe with a game of fetch, tug-of-war, or another classic.

Attention

All dogs love getting attention, but some more than others. If you see that your dog wants nothing more than being lavished with attention, you can actually use this as a reward for teaching it proper behavior. Wait for your dog to come to you for petting, but instead of immediately showering it with love, make it work for your attention. Give it a simple command like sitting down, and wait for it to do it. When your puppy finally does what it was told to, set aside some time for snuggling. If it doesn't do what was asked of it, step aside for 15-20 seconds, then return and try again. Shortly after trying this trick, your puppy will understand that completing the desired action means it is rewarded with hugs and smooches, so will be encouraged to behave properly and learn new commands.

Going Outdoors

Of course, this cannot actually be used for every *Sit* or *Stay* command, but at times, allowing your puppy access to the outdoors can also be used as a great reward to reinforce positive behavior. For instance, this can be quite beneficial when house training your pup. Put on the leash and take your puppy outdoors, to the spot where you like it to eliminate its waste. Do not let him sniff around and explore, but just wait for him to relieve himself. If your pup doesn't urinate, go back inside and try again later. When it finally relieves itself, praise it, and take it for a walk, allowing it to stop and explore as much as it likes. If your dog loves the outdoors, it will soon associate the spot for eliminating waste as access to the interesting sights and new smells, which will encourage it to relieve itself each time you bring it to that designated spot.

Giving your puppy treats seems to always do the trick, and this book will use that reward for the training sessions explained within. If you, for some reason, decide on another reward, the most important thing you need to have in mind is to reward your puppy immediately after it completes the desired action. Otherwise, the training will become an ineffective, long, and confusing process for both of you.

Home Sweet Home

Congratulations! You are about to add a new member to your family. But as eager as you may be to bring your buddy home, there are some things you need to tackle first in order to make sure that your home is not only appropriate for such a young pup, but also to help your pooch adapt to the new, strange environment. From what you should buy for your bundle of joy, how to organize your home so that it's safe for your puppy, to getting advice on making the first introductions, this chapter will help you get ready for your puppy's long-awaited arrival.

Shopping for the Essentials

My bet is, you have already spent some time online researching your puppy's breed to prepare for its arrival. But despite the fact that you have spent hours trying to write down a list of things that it will love, you have probably stumbled upon conflicting theories and different opinions. For some pups, such and such a toy was best, while others became aggressive at its sight. Some puppies preferred sleeping on a certain type of bedding, while others wanted to sleep on the floor tiles. You've read stories of how purchasing the most expensive crate will help you potty train your pup, but many also had a house training success with nothing but a gated corner in the kitchen.

Visiting a pet store doesn't help you clear your confusion either. With more choices than a toy store, shopping for your puppy's arrival can easily turn from exciting into daunting. So, what is the right choice? If you want to spare your budget (as well as your mind) from being blown, you should only stick to the essentials. Though you may be tempted to buy all sorts of different gadgets, leave that for later. Make sure that you have just the things your pup absolutely needs for the first couple of weeks. After you get to know your pup and discover its nature, the trip to the pet store will not be such a mind-boggling experience anymore, and you will know exactly what to buy.

Food and Treats

There are a lot of different types of doggy foods and treats. Although your puppy will probably be happy with pretty much anything that is made for puppies, you need to choose the right type depending on its breed and unique condition. Talk to its veterinarian and ask for advice. If your puppy has a special medical condition or food allergies, it goes without saying that you will have to be extra careful when purchasing its food and treats.

Bowls

Your puppy needs two bowls: one for doggy food and one for water. What you need to have in mind when purchasing bowls for your puppy, is their size and the material that they're made of.

Buy smaller bowls where your pup can easily reach its food and water. The best material choice is by far stainless steel, as it cannot break, it is heavy enough not to get knocked over every time it wants a sip, and it is the most durable. Ceramic bowls are not recommended because they can easily break. If plastic is your preferred choice, keep in mind that your pup will most likely chew on its bowl and make a mess, and there's also the chance of it developing a reaction that can cause nose discoloration.

Collar

Though you may want to reach for the one that you think looks best, when it comes to choosing a collar, the color and printed design is the least important factor you should look for. If planning on house training your pup, it is recommended for you to buy not one, but two collars:

Training Collar - Purchasing a special collar for the training practice is highly recommended. That way you can make sure that your puppy is easy to guide when on a leash, which will be much appreciated until your pup learns proper leash walking.

There are two types of training collars that you can choose from:

1. No-Pull Harness – This is a collar that goes around the puppy's chest instead of its neck. It is specially designed to discourage puppies from pulling on a leash. For safety reasons, this is the recommended option as it prevents from choking.

2. Martingale Collar – This collar is also called the *limited-slip* collar, as it prevents your pup to back out of it when it starts pulling. And if your dog has a longer neck, such as a Greyhound, for instance, this is by far the best collar option.

Buckle Collar – When you're not training your pup, it's better to leave a buckle collar on. The buckle collar should also have an ID tag attached, in case of emergencies. It is not recommended to be training your pup with a buckle collar on as you will not have the same amount of control as with a training collar. Besides, if your pup grows to be much stronger than anticipated, the training can become pretty inconvenient.

Leash

Whether leather, cotton web, or nylon, no matter what material the leash is made of, the important thing to look for when buying a leash is only the length. The perfect lash is 6-foot long, however, if you want to let your pup run around your backyard without you guiding your way, you can consider buying a long line (30-foot long).

Purchase the leash with the training process in mind. It is not about the strength, but about teaching with finesse. The leash should be light and easy for you to handle. Stay away from heavy and inconvenient chain leashes.

Crate

Do not let the cage-like look of the crate discourage you from buying one. Your pup needs a cozy, den-like space that is clean, enclosed, and most importantly, only theirs. The crate will be its place to rest and it will also help it feel safe while you are away. Think of the crate, not like a cage but more like a baby crib. You wouldn't leave your baby to sleep in the middle of a large, open, and unprotected room, right?

And just like with a baby's crib, buying a crate for your puppy is also not that simple. You will have many different options that come in different sizes, colors, and materials. Not to get too overwhelming, here are some tips that can help you find the perfect one for your pup:

- Before buying a crate, do some research and find out exactly how much your puppy will grow, in order to make the right choice.

- Keep in mind that your pup grows very quickly, so buying the smallest one may not be a perfect choice, unless you want to keep spending your money, that is. For best results, buy a size-adjustable crate that you can use while your puppy is still young, but also when he reaches adulthood.

- If you cannot find a size-adjustable crate, do not despair. Just shrink the space with the use of some pillows, since sleeping in a large crate will encourage your pooch to eliminate waste inside.

- If you plan on traveling a lot, buy a plastic crate for your convenience.

- If you're not traveling, stick to a wire crate. Despite their cage-like look, they do offer the best airflow and visibility and are therefore recommended.

Gate

Gates can be super beneficial if you have a staircase in your home that you want to block, keep your pup away from dangerous areas or an off-limits room, or simply if you want to close off a room to play with your pooch or even supervise.

Do not think that closing off space and gating larger areas is cruel. Quite the contrary. Puppies feel lonely and forgotten in large spaces, so providing an enclosed area for your pooch to play is recommended.

Toys

Puppies love bouncy and squeaky things. They don't care if it is red, green, or if it costs $1 or $15. But, despite the fact that your pooch will be satisfied with anything it can chew on, it is your job to offer only the quality toys.

And quality doesn't often mean expensive. When buying toys for your puppy, the most important thing for you to have in mind is for the toys to be appropriate and safe to chew on:

- Squeaky toys will keep boredom at bay and are great if you to want to be involved in the game

- Chew toys are perfect for mental stimulation and healthy gums. Just make sure they are appropriate for your pup

- You can also buy a rope, ball, or a Frisbee, for an interactive game

- Never let your pup play with tennis balls or sticks. These are not dog-appropriate toys and chewing on these can cause damage. Ask for advice on what toys are best for the size and breed of your pup.

Shampoo and Brush

Hygiene always comes first. And while you wouldn't have to bathe your puppy the first weeks of its life, having shampoo and a brush for him in your home, is essential. Tell the pet store salesperson what breed you are looking to buy a shampoo and a brush for and ask for some advice.

Puppy-Proofing Your House

Just like with toddlers, your house also has to be puppy-proofed, not only so that your puppy will not destroy your belongings, but most importantly so that you can prevent any injuries.

The average home is a real hazard for puppies, in most cases. Dogs are extremely curious animals by nature, and in order to prevent your puppy from chewing on something from under the sink or choking on a piece of wire, you need to secure your entire house before your pup gets home.

Here are some tips on how you transform your cluttered house into a puppy-safe environment:

Locked Cabinets and High Shelves. The very first thing you need to do is take all of the hazardous items, and place them somewhere where your pup cannot reach. The high shelves are perfect for this, and you can also lock up your cabinets to make sure that your puppy cannot get there. If the cabinets can be locked, perfect. If not, consider purchasing some childproof latches to increase security.

The items that you have to keep away from your pup include:

- Medication
- Plastic Bags
- Food Waste
- Cleaning Products and other Chemicals
- Cosmetic Products and Make-Up
- Children's Toys

- Valuable Items that You Don't Want to be Destroyed

Keep the Cabinets Closed. Besides locking up the cabinets, you need to adopt a habit of actually keeping them closed and locked. Rummaging through open cabinets is like searching for a mysterious treasure for puppies. To prevent your puppy from swallowing or choking on something, you need to keep everything closed. Appliances such as a dishwasher or washing machine should also be kept closed.

Keep Food Out of Reach. Most food items are also hazardous for your puppy. Food such as chocolate, onions, or coffee, can make your pooch really sick. Make sure to store your food properly and do not leave half-eaten things lying around your kitchen. The same thing goes for glasses.

Here are some tips on how to keep food away from your puppy:

- Store your fruits and veggies in hanging baskets.

- Secure your foods inside your pantry, fridge, and cabinets.

- Dog's food also has to be secured in a food container.

- Make sure to throw away wrappers and peels and keep them out of reach.
- Packaged foods should also be kept off of counters.

Keep Houseplants Away. You may not be aware, but most of the common houseplants actually present a hazard to your puppy. It is recommended that you check if your houseplants are toxic or not, and ultimately, keep all of your plants in hanging baskets or on a high shelf.

Organize the Wires. In most households, there can be found wires hanging out on every appliance. Many pups are actually drawn to these wires, and it really goes without saying how dangerous they can be for them. Make sure to organize the cords in your room and keep the wires tucked behind pieces of furniture. You can also secure your wires by gathering them up in a slack and then tying with a zip tie. Keep your chargers and portable electronic devices out of reach, as well.

Secure the Fireplace. The fireplace can also be a safety hazard. When your pup gets all excited chasing a ball or playing a fun game, it can easily fall into the fireplace. And since dogs can also experience tunnel vision when they are all wired up, you can see how dangerous this can be.

Installing a fireplace screen or a gate can be of great help. Fireplace gates can be found not only in the furniture stores, but in most well-equipped pet stores, as well.

Secure the Backyard. If you have a backyard, chances are, your pooch will be spending most of its time there. But, besides offering freedom, your yard can also pose a danger to your puppy.

Here are some tips on how to make it a secure and safe place for your puppy:

- Secure the gate. If you are planning on letting your puppy spend unsupervised time in the yard, the first thing you need to make sure is that your gate and fence are secure. Keep in mind that dogs are great diggers, so place some large rocks near the fence's base if necessary, so your pup cannot slip under.

- Do not use pesticides. If gardening is your hobby, make sure to keep your garden alive without pesticides, as most of them can make your pup really ill. When buying lawn and garden products, make sure to look for the "pet safe" sign written on the label.

- Keep the tools out of reach. Tools, as well as, smaller objects such as screws and nails, sharp things, and car parts, should be put on a shelf in the garage, or stored in a place that your puppy will not have access to.

- Clean anti-freeze. Anti-freeze is a real threat to dogs because it is extremely toxic, and dogs are attracted to its specific smell. If you believe that there might be some anti-freeze on the driveway or your garage floor, you will have to thoroughly clean that area, to prevent the puppy from licking it.

- Auto chemicals, rat poison, mothballs, and other poisonous things, should always be locked away and kept out of reach.

Getting Introduced

When it comes to bringing your pup home, the most important thing that you need to have in mind for that first day, is to let it be your puppy's day. Your pup is not just something you've brought home from the store. It is a living creature that feels things just as deeply as us humans. Try to keep your home absolutely stress-free for the first 24 hours at least, and reschedule all of your appointments.

-If you have kids, make sure to keep them calm (use tasty bribes if necessary). The point is to welcome your puppy the right way, not to get it all riled up so it starts nipping and jumping around like crazy.

A Welcome Circle

They say that first impressions are usually right. Make sure to give your puppy the best first impression. The important thing is for him to feel welcome and safe in its new home. For that purpose, you can create a welcome circle:

1. Have all of the family members sit on the floor, in a circle.

2. Give everyone a couple of doggy treats.

3. Create a circle with your legs, by spreading them out so your feet will touch.

4. Place your puppy in the middle.

5. Let everyone give the puppy a treat and pet it. If you have kids, make sure to teach him how to pet and hold your puppy properly, before it arrives home.

What About Other Pets?

Resident pets are, in most cases, not thrilled about sharing their living space with another animal. Small puppies tend to be annoying to other pets, and the attention oodles that your puppy may be getting can affect your other pet in a negative way.

It might take some time for them to get to know each other, so be prepared.

It may take a while for your pets to get used to one another, but there are some things you can do to knock down the tension a bit:

Introduce with Smell, First. Before you introduce the pets with each other, make sure to get them used to their smell, first. Animals are smell sensitive, and by getting them introduced with the smell of the other pet first, you lower the surprise effect when they actually get to meet.

Put the Resident Pets First. The puppy's reaction is important, but what's important is for it to feel welcome. For that purpose, you may need to keep jealousy at bay so that your older pets don't start taking their dissatisfaction out on the puppy.

There are several ways to do this:

- Feed them first
- When entering the door, greet them first
- If your older pet is also a dog, let it pass first (whether through doorways or when climbing stairs)
- If your older pet approaches you while you're interacting with the pup, turn away

from it for a minute and address the other pet instantly

- Treat and play with them first

Don't be afraid that your new pup will be said if it looks like you're giving most of the attention to the other pet. That way you will teach your puppy to grow into respecting the resident pet and to act accordingly.

Keep the Puppy in a Confined Area. If you think that there will be a lot of tension between the two pets, knowing the behavior of your resident pet, you should plan ahead about keeping the puppy in a confined area. If you, however, decide on a place where the older pet used to eat, make sure to change the feeding area, at least 7-10 days before your puppy arrives home.

For Cats, Let Them Introduce Themselves. If your resident pet is a cat, do not try to use force, but let it introduce itself in its own time. Whether it will be fearful or not, try to give it access to the area where your pup is, but, do not try to push it to enter the room. When your cat is ready to get closer to the puppy, let the cat wander around the room, but only at its own will. If your pup turns wild and starts acting like crazy, enter the room and try to calm it down.

Surviving the First Week

You've finally made it home! You may want to speed things up a bit and take your pup on a full tour of the house or put it on a leash and take it to the dog park, but don't let over excitement clout your judgment. Your pup is still young, and in its eyes, everything is brand new and confusing. Give it some time to adjust first. Take this slow the first week, so you can both adapt – your puppy to its new house, and you to your new family member.

The First Day

Although it is the most exciting, keep your expectations about the first day as low as possible. After all the anticipation, your pup is finally home, however, your introduction may not be what you've envisioned. Most dog owners have said that the first day is typically odd, so don't expect too much from your pup then.

On the very first day, pretty much anything can happen. Your pup may be overly excited and jumpy, it might just step right into the mix, or it may even be sleepy and a bit isolated. Whatever its reaction is, know that it is perfectly normal. After all, this is a brand new adventure for your puppy, and it may not feel prepared just yet. Give it time to adjust.

Enclose the puppy in a room the first day and supervise it at all times. Spend some time observing it and its reaction, and make sure to reflect its interests in a calm and positive way. The most important thing is not to overwhelm it right from the start, so it can get used to things easily.

Days 2-7

Unlike the first day, the rest of the first week will be pretty progressive. Even by day 2, you will notice changes in your pup's behavior, and it will most likely start accepting the situation (and the people) around it better.

Make sure to spend some time bonding and getting to know each other. Leave the training session for later, and just be with your pup. If it is chewing things, try to simply use a taste deterrent the first week. Again, do not overwhelm it. Be positive and talk to your puppy in a cheerful way.

The Food Dilemma

What should you give your pup to eat? How much should your puppy eat? What to use as a treat? These are all questions that new dog owners are most likely to ask themselves when thinking about adopting a puppy and training it to become an obedient adult dog.

Walking down the food dog aisle only makes things more complicated. Unlike back in the day when there were one or two types of dog food, today, the choices are pretty endless. But, that's a good thing. Specialized dieting formulas and high-quality foods with essential sourcing contribute to the overall health of your puppy.

But, despite the obvious reason why you should choose quality ingredients for your pup – which is providing your puppy with a balanced diet rich in essential nutrients, something else can benefit from balanced meals besides your puppy's health, and that is its training success.

Many dog owners overlook the importance that the food has over the process of training, but the truth is, even the simplest directions can take a lot of time to teach if your pup is under or overfed.

Your pup will be the happiest if it has a predictable feeding routine, so make sure to provide that. Besides the fact that it thrives when a consistent schedule has been set, the regular feeding times can also support the house training process. Knowing exactly when and how much your pup has eaten makes it a lot easier for you to determine its potty needs, which can be a lifesaver when training your puppy to accept his drop zone.

The Feeding Schedule

But just how much should your pup eat? Most new dog owners make the mistake of overfeeding their puppies, who then refuse to cooperate during the training session, and the whole process is one overwhelming experience. To avoid that, you need to set a consistent routine from the start. Here is a timeline for your puppy's first year. Stick to it.

6 to 10 Weeks – 4 feedings a day

10 Weeks to 4 Months – Decrease the feedings to 3 times a day

4 to 6 Months – 2 feedings a day

6 to 12 Months – After your pup has reached his 6th month, you can drop his feeding to one time a day

What to Feed and How Much?

There is a difference between dog and puppy food. Puppy food is specially formulated to meet the needs of young puppies and help them develop normally while providing all of the essential nutrients. Switching to adult dog food will only rob your pooch from these nutrients. Make sure to stick to puppy food throughout the first year.

And if you are wondering whether paying the big bucks really makes the difference, of course. If you can afford premium food for your puppy, know that you will be getting high quality and nutritional diversity in return. If you cannot, however, don't worry. Ask your veterinarian to give you advice on how to provide the best nutritional value for your pup.

As for how much to feed your pup, that really depends. Small breeds need, obviously, smaller portions than large puppies. But there isn't a set rule, really. The only thing you can do is to watch your pup closely, not his bowl. Through a trial and error, you will be able to determine the exact amount of food your puppy needs. If your puppy skips a meal here and there, or it picks at its food, that is usually a sign that you are either supposed to eliminate one feeding, or that you are simply giving him more food than necessary.

The Treats

The treats are the most important factor in the process of positive training. Without these tasty rewards, your pup will not be encouraged to participate in the sessions and go through all the trouble of getting your directions right.

But, what exactly is a treat? Should you pay tons of money for the most expensive smelly bones just for the sake of luring your pooch to show a shred of interest in the training? Of course, not. The treat can be pretty much anything your puppy loves to eat, even regular dog food. In fact, most dog trainers suggest that the treat should be a mixture of regular food and more special pieces of treats.

The most important thing is for the treats to be:

- Chewy
- Rich in Aroma and Flavor
- Easy to Break
- Soft

Start with a small number of treats and mix them up with doggy food. As the training progresses, increase the treats gradually. Also, make sure to use different treats on a weekly basis, so that your pup doesn't lose interest for cooperating. Treats can be pretty much anything your puppy enjoys – from special bone-shaped doggy treats, to small pieces of cheese or sausage.

House Training Your Puppy

House training is one of the very first things that you need to teach your puppy. It should be started the minute you bring your pooch home, but don't expect to reap the benefits too soon. House training a pup can be a long process, so if you aren't armed with the right amount of patience, you are in for some disappointment.

Puppies are stubborn, naughty, and they just love to push your boundaries. You need to be seriously committed if you want to succeed, and most importantly, to develop a consistent routine that will help your pooch learn.

The general rule of thumb is that puppies can be successfully house trained by the time they are 14-16 weeks old. If you have brought your puppy home with just 8 weeks, you can expect earlier results, sure. Just don't keep your hopes too high and remember that puppies don't really start learning until they reach their 12th week.

Regardless of your pup's current age, the guidelines of this chapter can help you have a housetrained pup in just a few weeks. As long as you obey the four house training rules, you will manage to create a healthy learning environment for your puppy:

1. Praise your pup immediately after it behaves

2. Keep a solid and consistent routine

3. Never punish your pup physically if it has an accident

4. Do not correct your puppy unless you catch it in the act

Getting Used to the Crate

The idea of being locked up is no more appealing to dogs than it is to humans. No one wants to have its freedom limited, so don't think that just because you've purchased an expensive crate your pup will fall in love with it the minute it steps inside. Chances are, you will have to train your pup to become used to its crate and love spending time there.

Many novices think of crate training as confining and not that natural, but the truth is, dogs are den animals by nature. They may not be thrilled about being locked up, that's for sure, but their instinct tells them that they should have a safe place of their own. Providing a crate is not cruel but comforting.

But, just because your pup doesn't perceive the crate as its safe spot just yet doesn't mean that you cannot change its point of view and make it realize that the crate is the perfect resting place for it. And since puppies have absolutely no preconceived notions, incorporating a few tricks in order to train your puppy to love its crate is indeed possible.

Assuming that you've already purchased the appropriate crate for your pup and that you got the size right, you can now follow these next steps to create your puppy's safe haven and get it to love it:

Step #1: Find the Perfect Spot

Many dog owners tend to overlook this one, which is exactly why they experience resistance and cannot crate train their puppies properly. You may think that the place where you'll put the crate doesn't really matter as long as it is dry and clean, but it can have a huge impact on how your pup is going to respond to its new home.

Imagine your family locks you up in the basement and they go upstairs to spend a lazy afternoon in the family room. How would you feel? No one wants to be isolated. Dogs are social animals by nature and they love to feel like they belong to the pack. Here, the pack is your family. So set some room aside and make sure that you put the crate someplace where you and your family spend most of your time during the day, such as the living room or the kitchen. Otherwise, the crate will only feel like an isolating punishment and you will never be able to train your pup to love it.

Step #2: Make It Comfortable

In order for your pooch to feel secure in its crate, it has to provide comfort. You can easily create an atmosphere that is more den-like for your puppy, by putting a blanket (or a towel) on the bottom, so that your pup can sleep comfortably in it. If you have bought a wire or a mesh crate, you can also find a breathable blanket to place over the top, so your puppy can have a space that is only theirs and where it can rest peacefully.

Keep in mind that if your pooch is very prone to chewing on things, it may find the bedding to be a perfect toy. If that is the case with your puppy, remove everything from the crate and do not add anything on the bottom of the crate. Wait until your pup matures a bit before you make a bed inside the crate for it.

Step #3: Show Enthusiasm

The more enthusiasm you show for the crate, the more excited your pooch will be. As you set up its safe haven, chances are, your puppy will come over to give it a sniff and explore it. Once it is close to the crate, get all excited and start saying positive things about the crate. It may seem silly to you, however, trying to trick puppies into giving their crate a try with a happy tone almost always does the trick. Just speak positively and wait to see if your puppy will get inside on its own. Do not force it to step into the crate as that will only help your puppy get more scared of it.

Step #4: Open the Door

Once the crate is all set up and your pup has had the time to explore it (even if only from the outside), it is time to start training your puppy to fall in love with it. Keep in mind that this is a slow and gradual process, so do not try to rush things.

Start by opening the door of the crate. The second the door is opened, start encouraging your puppy to go inside by saying positive things. It may not be so easily convinced to check it out at this moment, but know that that's perfectly normal. The crate is still perceived as a big, strange object in your living room, so give it some time to get used to it.

If you convince your pup to go inside, however, be sure to immediately praise and reward your puppy for it, and by all means, do not close the door of the crate when it enters it. That will only create a feeling of entrapment and get your pup all scared. You need to make sure that your puppy is comfortable and feels secure when inside before you can think about closing it in.

Step #5: Leave Treats and Toys Inside

If your pup doesn't show enthusiasm and isn't particularly interested in seeing what's inside the crate, try to encourage it to check it out by leaving some of its favorite doggy treats inside the crate. Start by placing the treats where your pup can reach them even without getting inside. It is perfectly normal for your pooch to just poke his head inside and get the treats – let him. Praise your puppy after doing so and keep placing treats inside, but leave them further and further inside the crate, each time, to try to lure your puppy inside. Just don't forget the most important part – praise and reward.

If your puppy is not responding well to treats, try the same trick with its favorite toy, or with a brand new one that it hasn't gotten the chance to explore and chew on just yet.

Step #6: Feed Him Inside

The point of crate training is to help your puppy get comfortable with spending time inside the crate. And to do that, it will have to actually spend some time inside. If it enters voluntarily to get its treats or toy from inside the crate, you have already made great progress. However, unless your puppy decides to lay down inside and play with its toy there, you will have to trick it into staying more than a second inside the crate. And the perfect way to do it is with food, of course.

Lure your puppy in with a treat or his toy, around meal time. Once it enters the crate, bring it its food bowl inside, and let it eat there. Keep the door open at all times, for the first couple of meals.

Step #7: Try Closing the Door

When your pup becomes comfortable standing and eating its meals inside the crate, it is time for you to start closing the door. Stay near the crate door so that it can see you, and while it is busy chewing its doggy food, close the door of the crate. The first couple of times, do it only for a minute or two, and gradually increase the time the door stays closed until your pup can stay inside with a closed door for 10 minutes.

Step #8: Try with Longer Stays

When your puppy has no trouble eating its meals inside the crate with the door closed, it is time to try closing it even when it's not meal time. Place a treat or a toy inside the crate and call your pup to the crate. It is recommended for you to have a command for this, such as "Kennel" or something you are comfortable with.

Encourage your puppy to get in, close the door, and then stand near the crate for the first 5-10 minutes. Then, leave the room for a minute or two. Come back to the crate and let your pooch out.

Repeat this a couple of times a day for a few days, gradually increasing the time your puppy stays inside the crate, as well as the time you spend outside the room.

Step #9: Leave the House

Once you manage to get your pup to stay inside the crate for 30 minutes straight, then it is time for you to actually crate him when you leave the house for a short outing. Of course, you need to do this only if your puppy is ready and shows no signs of distress when inside the crate.

So, take your dog out for a walk or play with it for a while to exercise it and get it tired. Put it in the crate along with its favorite toy or two and close the door. Remember, this is just the same as before. The only difference now is that you will not be in the next room, but you will actually leave your house. Make sure to leave without any fuss.

Step #10: Crate at Night

Just like you need your bed, your pup also needs its own place to sleep. The crate is not just for safety reasons. It shouldn't only be the place you put your puppy when you leave the house. It should also feel like its safe haven; a place designated for your puppy, where it can rest and sleep without being bothered. To help it understand that, you will also need to crate your puppy at night. It is strongly recommended that you put the crate in your bedroom at night, not only for practical reasons such as your puppy needing to pee during the night but also because being in the same room with you at night will help your pooch understand the whole concept of the crate better.

Step #11: Understanding How Long is Too Long

Keep in mind that your pup is a social animal who needs exercise on a regular basis. In order for it to be physically, as well as emotionally, healthy, your pooch needs regular activity. Leaving it locked up in the crate for too long can only create problems in its development.

Except at night, you should never leave your pup crated for longer than 5 hours. Here are some crate-time guidelines to help you understand just how long your puppy can be left in the crate during the early stages of its development:

9-10 Weeks – 30 to 60 minutes

11-14 Weeks – 1 to 3 hours

<u>15-16 Weeks</u> - 3-4 hours

<u>17+ Weeks</u> – 4+ hours, but <u>never</u> longer than 6 hours

Step #11: Know How to Respond to Whining

If you gave your child a chocolate bar every time it started crying, would you be raising them properly? Do not think that dogs are any different. If you do not set strict rules from the beginning, you will have serious behavior problems in the future. Pleasing the pup every time it starts whining is just like giving chocolate to a naughty three-year-old. Unless you believe your pup needs to eliminate waste, letting him out of the crate just because it is whining will have a counter effect on your crate training process. By letting your pup know that it can get more freedom if it starts whining, will only encourage this behavior and you will never be able to get your pup used to its crate.

Learning to Accept the Leash

Walking on a leash is one of the first skills that your puppy will master. Knowing leash etiquette is polite behavior that any pup should be taught from the very beginning. Proper leash manners are not only beneficial for practical purposes such as going to the groomer or having a veterinarian check, but they are also crucial for your pup's socialization and introduction to the world, in general. Knowing how to walk nicely on a leash will give your puppy more freedom to explore the outdoor wonders safely.

But, why is it important to start with leash training as soon as possible? Imagine your pup is from a larger breed. Before you know it, your small pooch will grow to be a strong and tugging tank that can pull the leash powerfully and even drag you over. This can be dangerous for various reasons. To avoid all that and provide security, your pup needs to accept the leash as early as possible.

Puppies don't know how to walk on the leash instinctively. They start pulling and get really uncomfortable once they feel the leash pressure. In order for you to avoid the leash training become a traumatic experience for your pup, you need to do it the right way.

Depending on your pup's temperament, there are three different methods in which you can introduce leash walking. Read on to choose the one that suits you and your pooch the most.

The Essentials

First of all, to get started with any of the three leash training methods, you will need 4 essential things:

1. The Collar – Your pup should have its collar around its neck in order for you to attach the leash. Make sure that the collar is comfortable around your puppy's neck and that it cannot slip out of it.

2. The Leash – For this purpose, you will need a non-retractable, regular leash.

3. The Treats – To reward and encourage leash walking, you will need tasty doggy treats. However, if your pup's a very food-motivated canine, you can use its regular food instead.

4. Patience – Keep in mind that you will need a lot of patience for this. You will need to stay calm when the puppy fights the leash and encourage proper behavior in a positive and encouraging tone. Avoid teaching leash walking when you are not in the best mood.

The Drag Method

If your pup is very young or timid, then you may find that you will need a bit more time for the drag method. That's okay! Let your pooch become accustomed to dragging its leash around before you take it a step further and decide to add pressure on the leash.

Step #1: The Collar

For you to be able to leash your pup, it has to wear its collar around its neck. Now, this probably sounds easy, but you will definitely experience resistance. Most puppies aren't comfortable with having something around their necks and they need time to adapt and get used to it. Allow it!

If you have trouble putting your puppy's collar on, follow these steps:

1. The best time to put your pup's collar on is when it is preoccupied with something else, like chewing on a rubber toy or munching on its favorite treat. Have in mind that the collar should be tightly fastened, but it should also feel comfortable. The rule of thumb says that you have fastened a comfortable collar if the collar is fastened just enough so you can slip two fingers underneath it.

2. Once the collar is on, leave it for about 10 minutes.

3. Then take it off and put it on again after 50 minutes.

4. Leave the collar on for 10 minutes at every hour, for about 2 days.

5. The third day, leave it on for 20 minutes instead of 10, again, at every hour.

6. Do this for 2 more days.

7. On the fifth day, leave the collar on at all times.

8. Leave it on for 3 days before introducing the leash.

Step #2: Attach the Leash

When your puppy is comfortable having the collar around its neck, it is time for you to attach the leash to it. Attach the leash and allow your pup to drag it around your home. Of course, shorter leashes work best for this practice, and if you have a special one without the handle to get caught on objects around your house, that would be perfect.

Step #3: Take It Outside

Go outside and allow your puppy to drag the leash there as well. Just make sure that you are keeping an eye on it. Let it drag the leash for about 4 days before taking the loose end of it. To avoid scaring your pup, do this in a calm and familiar location, such as your backyard.

Step #4: Explore

Let your pup explore while holding the loose end of the leash. Make sure not to apply pressure and let your puppy guide the way. Do this for about 10 minutes or so, and then encourage it to follow you inside, while still holding the leash loosely. If it refuses to follow you, do not drag him. Pick your puppy up and carry him inside.

Step #5: Do It Again

Over the next couple of days, take your puppy outside for at least 5-6 times. Hold the leash loosely and allow it to explore freely.

Step #6: Gentle Tugs

If you have taken your puppy outside for at least five to six times, then you are ready to apply gentle pressure to the leash. Go outside as you did before. Every three minutes or so, call your puppy in a positive tone. While doing that, gently tug the leash. If your puppy comes all encouraged and happy, praise it immediately and give it a treat. If it is not responsive and fights the leash, ignore it and wait until it stops. When it finally stops, repeat the process again. This may take longer for some puppies, but you need to have patience. The point here is for your pooch to associate the gentle tugs with positivity, so you can safely take him out for a walk.

Step #7: Practice

Practice makes perfect! Practice calling your puppy and rewarding it when it behaves, until it stops fighting the leash completely. Continue encouraging it to follow you with the leash as well as your voice, and you will have a leash trained pup in no time.

The Pressure Method

This is a bit more of an advanced, and quicker method. It doesn't include the drag routine, but it may not work if your puppy is still very young.

Step #1: The Collar and Leash

After your puppy is used to having its collar around the neck, attach its leash to it. Give it a treat after attaching the leash.

Step #2: The Tug

Once the leash is attached, pull a bit on the leash so that your pup can feel some pressure, but do not use too much force or drag your pup towards you. If your pup steps forward on its own after feeling the tug, even just a bit, praise it immediately and give it a treat.

If it begins fighting the leash, stand still and keep the leash tight. When the puppy finally stops, praise it, show it the treat, and then encourage it to come to you. When it does, give it the treat.

Step #3: Repeat

Repeat this until your pup begins coming towards you as soon as it feels the tug. Once it begins coming to you consistently, do not praise after just a few steps. Save the treat for after the pup has come all the way. Continue to praise with a positive and encouraging voice though.

Step #4: Practice

When your pup is used to come all the way to you whenever you tighten the leash gently, it is time for you to take things outside and start going out on real walks. Whenever your pup starts pulling ahead, simply stop or even change a direction so that your puppy can feel the tightening of the leash. Practice until your pup no longer pulls on the leash and follows you without any resistance.

The Wait Method

This method may take a bit longer, as you are practically doing nothing but waiting for your puppy to figure out on its own that it is supposed to come to you, but it can be extremely effective for some puppies. If the previous two methods don't quite work for you, give the 'wait' technique a try.

Step #1: The Collar and Leash

Just like before, your pup needs to be used to the collar in order to leash train it. If it is used to it, attach the leash to the collar.

Step #2: Hold and Stand Still

Take the leash with one hand and stand still. Do not move nor call your puppy. Even if it starts pulling, stand still and don't let go. The point here is to wait for the puppy to come to the end of the leash on its own. This may take a few minutes, so be patient.

Step #3: Praise and Reward

If your pup starts fighting the leash when it gets to the end of it, wait for it to stop. Once it does that, praise it immediately and reward with a treat. If it doesn't fight or pull, obviously, you praise and reward right away.

Step #4: Create a Slight Tension

Once your pup stops pulling and is no longer fighting the leash, take a step or two away from it, just enough for the leash to become slightly tighter and create a gentle pressure. If it starts fighting it now, wait for it to stop. Praise and reward when it does. Once you reward, release the tension immediately.

Step #5: Practice

Repeat it all for as long as it takes for your puppy to learn that feeling a slight tension around its neck means it should come to you, follow you, and eventually, walk nicely by your side.

Keep in mind that this is not the same as traditional training. You will not be pulling the leash for correcting your pup. You are simply teaching it to get used to sometimes feeling a slight pressure around its neck, in order to prevent unwanted behavior during one of its walks later on.

Potty Training

Although it may seem to you that puppies do nothing but chew on things all day long, believe it or not, their potty activities actually follow a pattern: eat → drink → rest (or move out of isolation) → play → chew. It is important for you to keep a close eye on your pup and take it outside after each activity in order to establish a healthy potty routine.

Even though this seems like a lot of potty runs and despite the fact that your 8-10-week old pup cannot really control its impulses, taking it to its drop zone often (even if inside the house) and letting it try to eliminate waste there will actually lay out the foundation of its understanding on how to "hold it in".

Time + Direction + Consistency

If you haven't had the opportunity to potty train a pup or a child, you are definitely in for some surprises. It takes a lot of effort, time, and it requires a well-established routine. It may take days, but it is also normal if it takes months to teach your pup where its drop zone is and how to control itself until it gets there. It will also require a lot of directions, as your puppy cannot read your mind. Even if it is house trained, you will still need to direct it and tell it what you want it to do. And finally, you will need to be consistent: where you will take it and when, what its behavioral signs are, and what your route will be like, are all factors that you have to consider (and stick to!) if you want to be successful.

Time + direction + consistency is the secret formula that will help you potty train your pooch.

Steps to Potty Training

Step #1: Understand Your Puppy's Breed Behavior and Needs

Not all dogs have the same needs. Before you get discouraged by your training failure, see what you have been doing wrong. Each breed has its unique needs or may also have special behavior that requires a different approach. For instance, if your dog is of a small breed such as Chihuahua, you should keep in mind that their small bladder will require them to urinate much more frequently than Bulldogs, for instance. Also, with smaller breeds, accidents are more likely to happen, even if your puppy is successfully house trained. So keep that in mind when establishing a routine.

Step #2: Choose a Potty Zone

Choosing a drop zone for your pup and teaching your puppy that that's the place where it can safely eliminate waste is of extreme importance, not only for you to have a well-behaved dog with healthy habits, but also to prevent your house from becoming an unsanitary environment.

But, how do you pick the right potty zone and what should you have in mind while doing so? Now, this really depends on your free time, needs, and personal preferences. The most important thing is for your puppy's bathroom area to be easy to clean and not visited by other dogs.

If your puppy is still young and hasn't received all of the necessary vaccines yet, it is recommended that you avoid areas that are too public, such as parks. Talk to your puppy's veterinarian and ask for their advice.

Step #3: Attach Leash and Accompany

Even if the drop zone is in your own backyard, a few feet away from your house, until your pup is trained enough to understand the whole concept of potty runs, you will have to accompany it to its bathroom area. Your pooch will also have to be leashed in order for you to be able to take it to the drop zone.

Step #4: Blaze the Trail

Most dog owners fail to potty train their puppies with success because they make one giant mistake – they do not follow the same path to the drop zone. Your puppy is extremely adaptive. It is a fast learner with a great memory. To make the process a lot easier, choose the same path to its potty area, at least until it is fully house trained. That means for you to go out through the same door, making the same turn, using the same bush, etc.

Another important thing is to never carry your pup to the drop zone, no matter how small (or slow) it may be. Your pup needs to be leashed and to walk on its own in order to learn how to navigate the path on its own.

Step #5: Use the Command Word Right

In order for you to be able to train your puppy to eliminate waste on cue, you will not only need to come up with a good command word, but you will also need to use it right. For instance, if you say "Go" when you reach the drop zone but your puppy is not showing any sign of being ready to urinate, you are only diminishing the power of the word. If you want your pup to understand what "Go" or "Get Busy" or whatever command word you choose means, you need to use it whilst the dog is eliminating waste.

So, once you get to the drop zone, stand still. Do not move and do not interact. Simply wait for your puppy to do its business as soon as you see it relieving itself, firmly say the command word. Repeat every time, for as long as it takes for your pup to learn, eventually (usually after a month or so), your pooch will be able to go on cue.

Step #6: Praise and Reward

Once your pup eliminates waste, praise it immediately. Say "Good Boy" or whatever praise word you have chosen and reward it with a tasty treat. This will help your pooch associate eliminating waste with praise and reward, kick-starting the potty-training process, and helping it learn quicker.

Establishing a Potty Schedule

Potty training your pup may seem like a lot of work, but once you are able to determine when your pup needs to go, it will be a lot easier for you. Of course, there is the previously mentioned eat-drink-rest-play-chew routine, but unless you know approximately how many times a day your pup needs to go potty, all of the behavior-tracking and taking-notes process will have very little meaning.

Well, exactly how many potty breaks does your puppy need? In the beginning, keep in mind that you will have to take your pooch outside every hour or two, as very young puppies need to go more frequently.

Here are some general guidelines that can help you with potty training:

<u>6 to 14 Weeks</u> – 8 to 10 times a day

<u>14 to 20 Weeks</u> – 6 to 8 times a day

<u>20 to 30 Weeks</u> – 4 to 6 times a day

<u>30 Weeks and Older</u> – 3 to 4 times a day

Based on the guidelines above, your pup's breed, as well as its unique condition, you need to set up a potty schedule.

Here is an example that a dog owner who works outside of their home can use:

Early Morning - Go Outside

Breakfast – Go Outside after Breakfast

Lunch Break Feeding – Go Outside

Midafternoon – Young Puppies Should Go Outside

Home from Work – Go Outside

Dinnertime (between 5 and 6 pm) – Go Outside

7:30 p.m. – Remove Puppy's Water

Before Going to Bed – Go Outside

Middle of the Night – Go Outside, if necessary

Keep in mind that your pup needs regular exercise, so if your work prevents you from providing that, consider hiring a dog walker. Just make sure to let your walker know your rules and schedule, in order to keep the training process on the right track.

Potty When Alone

The schedule above is a great example of how you can organize the potty breaks, but if you think that it's a magic bullet that will help your pup to hold it in while you're gone, you are so wrong. Remember, the puppy's bladder is a muscle that develops last. It fills up very fast, and before your pooch reaches social maturity, which happens around month 5, your puppy will have the urge to go a lot more than you probably want it to. Asking your pup to wait a while until you get back from work is just not going to happen.

If you cannot find a good solution for this, you can consider purchasing a playpen for your pooch. Let the playpen be for alone time for your puppy where it can both, sleep, and eliminate waste. Have a playpen that is large enough for your pooch to sleep in on one side and go potty on the other side.

First, make sure that that the playpen is made of a material that is non-absorbent and that is easy to clean. Place your pup's bedding and toys on one end of the playpen. Cover the remaining space with absorbent pads where your pup can go potty. Chances are, your pooch will eliminate on the pads, which can be quite handy.

The minute you get home, take your pup outside. Do not offer access to the playpen when you are home. Also, do not use the crate for this purpose. You need to teach your pup that the crate is for sleeping and resting only. If you encourage eliminating waste there, you will never be able to get it back on the right track again.

Use this technique for the first few weeks, if the pup needs to go potty more times than you can take him outside. Once it matures a bit and can control its urge better, you should stop putting it in the playpen. Crate him regularly instead.

Handling Accidents the Right Way

You have a small puppy in your home – messy carpets and potty accidents are pretty much part of the deal. It will be a while until your puppy is fully house trained and mature enough to control its urge to go. Smelly accidents are inevitable, but how you approach these situations can also have a huge impact on how successful the house training process will be.

When you catch your young puppy in the act of eliminating waste, the best approach is to try to take its mind off of it:

1. When you see your puppy relieving itself on the floor, startle it immediately. Saying "Ep, ep", jumping up and down, or clapping your hands may do the trick.

2. Once your pooch is interrupted, attach its leash and take it to its drop zone immediately. Now, your pup may not have the need to go now since it has probably already eliminated on the floor, but that's not really the point here. What's important is to teach your puppy that urinating or

defecating in the house is not allowed and that its drop zone is the safe place to do it.

3. If your pup manages to relieve itself, however, praise it like crazy for being good, and reward it immediately.

Keep in mind that you need to startle, but not scare your pup when you catch it in the act. The intent is to get your puppy's immediate attention. To help it understand and remember that what it is doing is wrong, it is recommended for you to use the same word, catchphrase, or make the same noise every time.

Do not punish your pup for eliminating inside. The old book says you should make it sniff its urine and slap it on the nose with a rolled newspaper, but besides being cruel, this can have a counter effect. In that situation, your puppy will only learn that it's unacceptable to eliminate waste and will most likely try to do it somewhere where you cannot reach easily so that it won't get punished again.

Tips for Successful Potty Training

Here are some tips that can help you potty train your pup better and faster:

<u>Watch the Water Intake</u> – Young puppies drink more water if they are bored or nervous. Make sure your pup gets enough exercise, and monitor its

water intake closely. Give it access to its water bowl around meal times and when you believe it is thirsty.

Remove its water bowl after 7:30 p.m. If your pooch wants to have a drink after that, give it a small amount, no more than half a cup, or even better, give it a few ice cubes for it to play with and keep thirst at bay.

Limit its water intake to prevent excessive urination, however, be careful not to dehydrate your puppy. If it is panting or becoming lethargic, offer it its water bowl immediately.

<u>Lay off the Treats</u> – The treats play a huge part in training your puppy with positive reinforcement, however that doesn't mean that you should give them sporadically throughout the whole day. If you treat your pooch more than you should, it will most likely start pooping a lot more in the house, and its habits for elimination will become random.

Try to give smaller treats and reward only when training, if possible.

<u>Clean Up the Accidents Privately</u> – It is a mistake for you to let your puppy see you clean up its elimination accidents. That way you send it the wrong signals and you are almost encouraging that action by offering it a nurturing-like acceptance.

When your puppy makes a mess, take it to another room or isolate it until you get the mess all cleaned up.

<u>Neutralize the Odor</u> – It is a common knowledge that dogs have a very strong sense of smell. Being an excellent sniffer, your pup will most likely return to eliminate waste where the smell of its urine is concentrated. Even if you cannot sense it, yes. For that purpose, make sure to always neutralize the odor of your pup's urine after an accident. Purchase an odor neutralizer from your nearest pet store, or even make your own solution by mixing an equal amount of water and vinegar and adding a few drops of essential oils to it. Place it in a spray bottle and, after cleaning, spray the area where the puppy has eliminated waste, to neutralize the smell.

Training Through Puppy's Growth Stages

Now, let's turn you into a proper trainer. This chapter is what you have signed up for when hitting the "buy now" button. It covers the basic directions and teaches the commands that puppies must learn in order to feel like an integrated part of the human world. Through the power of the word, you will be able to establish a communication bond like no other. Training your puppy is not just about turning it into an obedient dog. It's also about fostering mutual understanding for a lasting relationship.

Depending on the dog type, as well as the unique personality of your puppy, the training process can either be short and super effective or it may require some extra effort. Once you begin the practice, you will also learn that some commands are a breeze to teach while others have to be repeated dozens of times. Do not fret! Approach the training with the thought that you are actually teaching English words to another species. A certain amount of patience is indeed required.

The training sessions are divided and organized with the growth stages of your puppy in mind, for your convenience. From its early infant stages guiding you all the way to its adulthood, this chapter will help you master the basic commands and teach your puppy order and discipline with love.

8 to 12 Weeks

After the weaning period is over, which happens somewhere around week 7, your puppy is ready to be socialized and introduced to your family. If you still haven't adopted your puppy, make sure to do it when it has reached its 8th week. The weaning period is extremely important for baby puppies not only because the mother provides essential antibodies that will protect the puppy's health for many weeks to come, but also because those pups that stay with their mother throughout this period learn the doggy language and bite inhibition much better. If your puppy has been separated from its canine family way too early, it may be much more insecure around its new human family.

After your puppy is introduced with your family, it is only natural to want to teach it basic directions and train it to be disciplined. However, keep in in mind that the period before the 12th week is called the *infant period* for a reason. Your pup is just like an infant baby. It may be capable to learn a few things here and there, but its brain is not fully developed yet. That being said, don't expect too much from a puppy that's not 12 weeks old. You can start with the basic stuff but keep your expectations low.

Say Its Name

Your puppy may not be ready for some more advanced training sessions yet, but it's definitely never too early to start teaching it its own name. Use its name as often as you possibly can. When playing with it, when offering it a treat, or when you are simply praising or petting it. If you want to, you can also use a nickname that will highlight the cheerful moments and help your puppy associate its name with your positive attention. This can help you later on during the training process, as hearing its name will mean spending some fun time with you.

Just make sure to use a sharp but positive tone when calling to your puppy. Avoid sing-songs or speaking gibberish to your puppy just because it is a cuddly little thing. It may be just an infant and cannot fully grasp what's going on around it, but this is the perfect time for you to set the training basis. If you fail to teach your puppy how to respond to its name the minute you bring it home, you will need to work harder later on.

Get Them Used to the Leash

It is too early for you to introduce your puppy to the wonders of the dog park or the nearest beach. But just because you cannot take it for a walk around your neighborhood doesn't mean that you shouldn't get it used to the leash.

Put the collar on your puppy immediately after you bring it home. It will most likely fuss at first, but that's okay. Eventually, it will get used to it. If it has trouble accepting it, try the exercise from Chapter 5. Once it is comfortable with wearing its collar around its neck, it is time for you to attach the leash on it. Let it drag it around for a day until it gets used to it. After a day or so, you can pick up the leash and follow it around. As it becomes comfortable with you following it around, you can start calling its name and begin encouraging it to follow you.

If your pup is not particularly interested in strolling around your living room with you, try to do something to gain your puppy's interest. Foolish things always seem to do the trick. When it responds and begins following you, quickly say *"Follow"* and praise it by kneeling to offer a hug.

If it is too stubborn to accept the leash and collar, do not despair. Maybe your pup is just not ready at this stage. Keep in mind that your puppy is not 12 weeks old yet. Do not push it too hard. Drop everything and give it a try another day.

"Sit" and "Okay"

Although this stage is best for cuddling and spending quality time with your cute pooch, that doesn't mean that you cannot lay out the training basis. And working on simple commands such as *sit* and *okay* makes the perfect training foundation:

Grab a treat in your hand and show it to your puppy. It will probably get too excited and jumpy. That's okay. Do not force it into anything. Just slowly lower the hand with the treat to the floor, to see if you can lure it into a sitting-position. As you are lowering the hand, firmly say **"Sit"**.

1. Most puppies will most likely just lower their heads. See if you can use your other hand to gently show your puppy what it is supposed to do. Be careful, do not push, squeeze, or press too hard. Simply position your puppy by touching its waist muscles below its ribs so your puppy will know that it is supposed to sit.

2. This may take longer than expected, and that's perfectly okay. Keep in mind that you are trying to teach a baby to sit. Be patient and do not despair if your pup cannot quite

figure out what is expected of him. If it manages to sit down, give it the treat immediately, as a reward.

Do not expect too much from the "Sit" command just yet. Introduce it just to help your pup accept the training routine easier. You can start training your puppy to sit much more intensively, once it is at least 12 weeks old.

The infant period is the perfect time for you to start using a happy and encouraging word. Most trainers choose "Okay" as a positive command to give their pup permission, however, "Good Boy/Girl" or any other positive word of choice will do just fine. Help your puppy associate this command with good behavior and positive things. For instance, when it sits down on its own, say **"Okay"**. When it takes your treat or starts eating its meal, repeat this command. Give it a toy and say **"Okay"** just before it starts chewing on it, to help it understand that saying this positive command means giving it permission to complete what's on its mind.

Walking the Stairs

Stairs are known to probably be the most intimidating obstacle that young puppies are faced with. This is especially the case with smaller breeds that just aren't built to tackle the stairs just yet. Even if you have a bigger puppy that can walk up and down the stairs at this stage, keep in mind that most young puppies have a type of *stair phobia* as they are too young to determine just how much they can and cannot handle, as their depth perception has yet to be developed.

If you have stairs in your home, this is the perfect time for you to start encouraging your puppy to use them. Lower yourself to its position and gently cradle its belly while guiding its paws up and down the stairs. If even this is too frightening for your puppy, have another family member cheer your pooch from a few stairs away, to give it the encouragement to start moving its paws more freely.

Handling

Fear is a common occurrence in puppies that haven't reached 12 weeks of age. In fact, most trainers refer to the '8-12 weeks' stage as the *fear imprint period.* Fears and unpleasant experiences that occur before the 12th week seem to leave a much more lasting impression on puppies. Young puppies are often afraid of humans. If you fail to provide proper handling, your puppy may grow into a fearful dog that is wary of people.

Handling is a very important part that you as a puppy owner should take care of immediately after bringing your puppy home. This will not only help your pooch accept you much faster and jumpstart the training method, but it will also be much appreciated during veterinarian visits.

Handling can be done only when your puppy is calmed. Do not by any chance try to force handle, as that will have a counter effect. Instead, lay down on the floor with your puppy and as you are calmly petting it, perform a routine check-up. Peek into its ears, hold its head gently and look deeply into its eyes, handle its paws like you are trimming the nails, touch the base of your puppy's tail, and press the belly gently. Playing veterinarian will not only be fun, but it will also get your pup used to the human touch and become unafraid of handling.

To avoid scaring your puppy, praise it with hugs and reward with treats while handling it.

Socializing

Puppies at this age shouldn't be taken outside for a walk, but that doesn't mean that they cannot be introduced to your close friends and family. The period before the 12th week is the perfect time for you to begin the socialization process, as that will help your pooch adapt to new people and unfamiliar situations easily. So, in order to help your puppy, grow into a confident and well-adjusted dog that is comfortable around people and other dogs, you will need to expose it to strangers as early as possible.

Invite your friends and neighbors over (if you can invite some active kids over that would be perfect) or if possible, have a play date with another healthy dog. The important thing about early socialization is to help your pup build confidence and become familiar with uncertainties. Ask your guests to offer treats and handle your puppy gently in order for your pup to be as comfortable as possible. Have it near you at all times to keep the discomfort at a minimum., and to let it know that you are always by its side. When people approach your puppy and want to pet it, take advantage of the "Sit" command and encourage it to be calm while bracing it into a sitting position gently and giving it its favorite treat afterward.

Practice Food Conditioning

It is in a puppy's nature to protect what's theirs, so do not be surprised if your pooch develops a food or object guarding habit. Most puppies guard their food bowls or their toys and objects from other dogs but know that your pup can be just as defensive to your approach as well.

However, if you start with early food conditioning, you can prevent this mindset and eradicate food guarding from your pup's development.

1. Every other day when your pup is having a meal, go to it.

2. Offer it a biscuit or another doggy treat when it is halfway finished with its meal. Pat it on the head and say **"Good Boy/Girl"** or **"Okay"**.

3. When it accepts the treat, slowly take the food bowl away from it. Make sure to do this while your pup is still eating the biscuit.

4. After it has finished eating the treat, wait 10-15 seconds before returning the food bowl to it. Pat it on the head, and give it the **"Okay"** command again.

Make sure to involve all family members in this exercise, especially if there are children in the house. Food conditioning should be executed by everyone who shares the same roof with your puppy in order to avoid your pup developing the need to guard and protect its belongings from others.

12 to 16 Weeks

If you have a child, then you know that the second year of their life is called *terrible twos* for a reason. They become sneaky little creatures, using your weaknesses to their advantage. But what you probably didn't know is that the second puppy growth stage (the infant period doesn't count) also shares the same name.

During this, terrible second phase, your pooch is starting to realize what behaviors get your attention, what gets it the yummiest treats, and who is the boss. And yes, in your puppy's eyes, you may not be the person in charge. It may be your four-year-old daughter who gives it biscuits when no one's looking.

Even though you may think that your puppy is confident and pretty independent, the truth is, your puppy craves direction. If you let your pup run around without correcting misbehavior and teaching the right way, you will have a lot on your hands later on. The tips and tricks in this section will help you teach basic commands to a 12-month old puppy and guide your pooch through this terrible and pretty insecure period.

Keeping the Control

Giving your puppy complete freedom just because it is indoors is a terrible mistake. Being free to do whatever it wants means misbehavior, and misbehavior results in you paying for it – literally, by fixing broken furniture, and by investing more time and effort in future training.

Not to mention that an unsupervised puppy can be a danger to itself. Because, let's face it, no matter how doggy-proofed your house may be, your puppy will always find a choking hazard to chew on.

Keep in mind that your puppy is still pretty young, so you have to have your eyes on it most of the time. Here are some tips on how to keep your pup near you:

- Let it sit in an enclosed area where you can observe it easily. A gated kitchen is just one example.

- If you have bought a special crate of the right size for your puppy, you can keep it there whenever you cannot keep your eyes on it. Just remember to give it some toys to chew on, to keep boredom at bay.

- Make sure it is near you all the time, by attaching it to a leash. If you are dealing with a super active puppy that cannot be calmed that easily, then perhaps attaching it to a dragging lead will help you keep a constant eye on your puppy.

Just remember to praise and treat your puppy whenever it is confined, to encourage good behavior.

The TEN Basics

It may seem to you like your puppy understands nothing but food and chewing on chairs, but at this stage, your pooch has the capacity of having a ten-word vocabulary. Think of your puppy now as a toddler who can absorb knowledge but only if it interests them. It can learn a lot at this stage, but your bundle of joy is very much vulnerable to your impressions. Before we start with the ten basics, let's make sure you know how to start the training process the right way:

- Stay cool. Even if you have to repeat a single command dozens of times, do not get frustrated, or at least, don't let your pup see it. If you get impatient, that will only scare your puppy which will make it lose interest and become less responsive to the training sessions.

- Give clear and single directions. Be firm and make sure to enunciate the syllables. Repeat the command once, with the right tone and level of firmness. Keep in mind that a firm DOWN sounds a lot different than down-down-down-oh-come-on-puppy-please-get-down.

- Keep in mind that the pup is still very young, so give the directions when the puppy is in the right mood, which is usually during playtime and when your puppy is not hungry.

- Use your hands to signal and give visual directions if needed.

- Do not forget to immediately reward the pup after completing the task.

#1: Buddy's Name

The very first word that most puppies learn is their name. If you have already managed to get your puppy to come to you or react when it hears its name, you can check this off your list. But if your pooch is too stubborn or lazy to cooperate, you may need to teach it that when you say your puppy's name, that means "I am talking to you and I want you to pay attention".

When you call your pup by its name, it should be a cue for them to drop everything, turn towards you, and give you its full attention. If your pup is not quite responsive, it might be because you have been using its name the wrong way. The puppy's name should have one single meaning – attention. If you are using it as a correction or you are shouting it in an angry tone when you get mad at them, you are sending it confusing signals. To your pup, its name might mean three things:

1. Come to me now and give me your attention.

2. You are being very naughty and I am telling you off.

3. Come now, boy/girl. No? Now, I am angry.

Before you can actually teach your pup to respond whenever it hears its name, you need to first stop associating with negative things. Otherwise, you are only confusing your dog and making it harder for it to determine how it should respond to the sound of its name.

Step 1: Get Buddy's Attention

Before you begin, make sure that it is just you, your puppy, and a bag of treats. In order for it to learn, you need to make sure that there isn't anything that can distract it. Now, say its name in a warm tone, but make it sound firm. If you get no response, say it again, but this time, clap your hands or do a kissing noise to get its attention.

Step 2: Reward Immediately!

As soon as your puppy gives you its attention, mark the desired behavior with a positive word. You can use **"Good Boy/Girl", "Okay", "Yes",** or whatever works for you. The important thing is to <u>tell</u> your pup that it has done something good. Immediately after saying the word, give your pup a treat to reward its good behavior.

Step 3: Repeat

Repeat this for as long as it takes until your puppy is able to give you its full attention no matter what. To do so, you first need to get its attention when it is not distracted, and gradually increase the distractions to make sure that your pup will be responsive even in the most distracting situations. Toys and biscuits are perfect distractions. Try to give it access to some, and then start with step 1 and step 2.

#2: Look Up!

Whether you manage to get your puppy to look at you when it is preoccupied with something else or not, in the most distracting situations, you will need more than just a glance. You will need to get your puppy to pause whatever it is doing and really focus on you. This is how you can train it to pay a bit more attention when you need it to:

1. Pick a moment when your pup is not tired, not hungry, and when there aren't too many distractions around.

2. Grab its favorite toy or a treat that you know it loves.

3. Stand above and call your puppy's name as you lift the toy or treat upwards, from its eyes to yours.

4. Keep the toy or treat in that position for 2 seconds.

5. Say a positive word such as **"Good Boy/Girl"** to mark the behavior, and then give it a treat as a reward.

6. Make a small pause and then repeat this exercise, only this time, keep the toy/treat near your eyes for 5 seconds. Mark, reward, and then repeat again. With each repetition, increase the time it must stare at you (from 2 to 10 seconds).

This exercise will train your puppy to give you more than a second of its attention when it becomes distracted.

#3: Follow!

Training your puppy to follow you is one of the first and most basics commands that your pooch should learn. In the beginning, it is recommended that you do this on the go, meaning that you should try to instill a habit to *follow* when you are walking your pup on the leash:

1. Fill your pocket with doggy treats.

2. Attach the puppy's leash to his collar.

3. As soon as you take the first step, say the word **"Follow"** in a firm, but friendly way.

4. If your puppy starts walking alongside you, mark the behavior and give it a treat. If it isn't too enthusiastic about it, see if you can encourage it by showing it the treat.

5. Encourage your puppy to follow you with treats, while saying the command **"Follow"** every couple of seconds.

6. Once it begins cooperating, start increasing the length between the treats.

Once you get your puppy to follow you when on the leash, you need to take this training session a step further and get your puppy to learn that follow should mean follow, even if there is no leash involved:

1. When the leash is not attached to your puppy, fill a treat cup with treats and show it to them.

2. Start walking and immediately say the word **"Follow"**.

3. If your pooch starts walking towards you, give them a single treat when it comes to you. If it is not too excited, shake the treat cup to try to boost their enthusiasm.

4. Again, repeat this a couple of times and lengthen the distance between the treats.

In most cases, this exercise works like a charm, and most puppies are able to learn the "Follow" command in a relatively short amount of time. However, it is not uncommon for dog owners to stumble upon resistance. If your puppy doesn't want to move even after being lured with treats, it is important for you to be able to keep your cool. Do not be tempted to drag them. Besides the fact that it can cause physical discomfort, it can also scare them and make the whole process a lot harder. Persuading them to follow you is also not an option as by doing so you will be only be reinforcing their resistance. Instead, what you should do, is get creative. What interests your pup the most? Jump around, squeak a toy, kneel down, or do something that you think will be able to encourage your puppy to follow you.

#4: Sit

"Sit" is probably the biggest sign that the puppy is well-behaved. Like a child that knows how to say "Please" when asking for something. It is one of the best dog's manners, and it lasts a lifetime. Teaching puppies to sit is also one of the most basic commands, and it is a lesson that most puppies master in no time. Here is a simple exercise that if done properly a couple of times a day, it can be easily taught in just 4 days:

1. Grab a couple of treats in your hand.

2. Bring your hand slowly to your puppy's nose. Allow them to sniff it just to realize what you are holding, but do not give them the treats just yet.

3. Put one of the treats between your thumb and index finger.

4. Say **"Sit"** as you bring the treat above the puppy's nose, about an inch or so apart. Move the treat hand so you can lure them into a sitting position.

5. Once your pup is seated, mark the good behavior by saying **"Okay"** or **"Good Boy/Girl"** and give them the treat.

6. Repeat this exercise until there are no more treats left in your hand.

Keep in mind that in order for this to work, the treat has to be placed just about an inch apart and kept right above the nose. Why is this important? Because if you hold your hand too high, your puppy will be encouraged to jump, and if you keep it too low, they will most likely just take it and not even try to sit down. Above the nose, and an inch apart is a perfect position.

As easy as teaching this command may seem, with some puppies, you may need a more 'manual' approach. If your puppy doesn't want to sit down and refuses to cooperate at all, you need to help it understand what is asked of them and physically get it into a sitting position:

1. Have your puppy on your left side, both of you facing the same direction.

2. Kneel down. If your puppy is of a smaller breed, you can place it on a chair or table for your convenience.

3. Place your right hand against its chest and your left one on the pup's shoulders.

4. Firmly say **"Sit'"** and gently run your left hand over your puppy's shoulder, putting enough pressure to get them in a sitting position. By doing so, you will get your pup to sit on your hand.

5. When it is finally sitting on your hand, praise it with **"Good Boy/Girl"** and immediately give it a treat.

6. Repeat this exercise a couple of times, twice a day, for about 4 days.

#5: Down

"Down" is one of those ultimate cues. It literally means "Stop whatever it is you are doing this instant and lay down". This command can be a real life-saver when having guests over, especially if you are dealing with an overly cheerful and jumpy pup.

Introduce the "Down" command after your pup can sit when asked to, as this training session requires the puppy to know how to sit down on command.

This may be a bit trickier than "Sit", but "Down" can be mastered just as fast. Simply follow the steps below:

1. Take your puppy aside and grab some treats in your hand.

2. Instruct your pup to sit down. If you are still using the treats to lure it into a sitting position, it is best to leave teaching the "Down" command for after your pup learns to sit down without being tricked into that position.

3. Once your puppy is sitting on the floor, drop your treats on the floor, close to its paws, and immediately cover them with your hand.

4. Wait for a second to see the pup's reaction. If your puppy lays down on their own, say

"Down" the second it gets down, and give it one of the treats immediately.

5. Repeat these steps until there are no more treats left. Do this exercise for as long as it takes until your puppy learns how to get down when told.

If your puppy gets down on its own, you are one lucky dog owner, as most pups struggle with this exercise and need some assistance. If your pup is unsure what it is supposed to do, you may need to get them into a "Down" position yourself:

1. Just press them gently between their shoulder blades to get them into this position. While doing that, say **"Down"** firmly.

2. Once your puppy's elbows hit the floor, mark the good behavior by saying **"Good Boy/Girl"** or **"Okay"** or whatever positive cue you have chosen, and give them a treat immediately.

3. Repeat this a couple of times until your puppy learns that it is supposed to get down on its own. Then, you can follow the steps from above.

6: Stand

There are times when this cue will be deeply appreciated. Imagine you have just gotten back from outside and your puppy's paws are all muddy. If your pup knows what "Stand" means, you will have no trouble wiping dirt off your pooch's paws. Not to mention that grooming will be a breeze.

Here is how you can teach your puppy to stand:

1. Grab a doggy treat and place it between your thumb and index finger.

2. Place the treat about an inch apart from your puppy's nose.

3. Say **"Stand"** firmly, and immediately lift your hand up as if you were pulling a string from your puppy's nose.

4. Once your puppy is standing, start cradling its belly with your hand as you repeat **"Stand"**. This will teach your pooch that "Stand" means getting into that position and staying there until it is told otherwise.

5. Make a 2-second pause and then say **"Okay"** or **"Good Boy/Girl"** to praise the good behavior, while giving them their reward – the yummy treat – immediately.

6. Repeat these steps with a couple of treats, a few times a day.

Now, in the ideal scenario, your puppy will be able to stand and hold that position for as long as the treat is in front of them. But, in most cases, young pups are impatient and try to snatch the treat from your hand. If your puppy is like that, just make sure to hold the treat firmly, and use a cue that will discourage them such as **"Ep, ep"**. Dealing with an impatient pup may require some extra effort, but the steps from above will surely help you teach your pooch to stand.

#7: Give

Puppies at this stage are just like two-year-olds. They love to play with toys, but the whole concept of sharing is not familiar to them. It is your job to teach your puppy that it is supposed to share. Mastering this command will be especially appreciated when your pooch finds something dangerous to chew on when out for a walk.

Here is how you can teach your puppy to give:

1. Find a toy that your puppy likes to play with and have it near you. Put a couple of doggy treats in your pocket, as well.

2. Kneel down on the floor and spend a minute or two praising your pooch and petting it happily, before you bring out its toy.

3. Now, take its toy, toss it in the air, and catch it yourself. This is done so you can pique your puppy's interest and make them want to play.

4. Then, toss it again, only this time, give it just a short toss so that your puppy can catch it.

5. If your pup takes the toy, let them have it for a minute or two. Do not try to take it away from them immediately, as it is important for them to feel that you're not challenging them.

6. Now that it has had its fun, bring out the doggy treat. As you offer it the treat, it is supposed to spit out its squeaky toy and take it. As it does that, firmly say **"Give"** and take the toy with your hand.

7. Praise them by saying **"Good Boy/Girl"** or **"Okay"**.

8. Once it has eaten the treat, give it back its toy. This is very important, as it will highlight your good intention. Otherwise,

your pup may associate this action with you stealing their possessions.

9. Repeat steps 4,5,6, and 7 until your puppy understands the game. If it looks at you immediately after it picks up his toy, that means that it is ready to "Give".

There are a couple of things that may cause you trouble with this exercise:

1. First, your puppy may run away from you the second it sinks its teeth into the toy and try to get its squeaky friend to the nearest corner. If that is the case, try again, but this time, keep your puppy on a short leash.

2. The other thing that can be tricky, is if your puppy simply refuses to release the toy. When that happens, simply squeeze their upper muzzle, behind their canine teeth. Once it releases the toy, praise them and reward as usual. The point is for your puppy to understand how to play this game and learn that "Give" means releasing.

#8: Settle Down

The period between 12 and 16 weeks is the perfect time for you to teach your puppy to settle down and go rest in their specially designated area. Just make sure that your puppy is actually older than 12 weeks, in order to avoid them feeling entrapped and insecure, as they cannot fully grasp the "Settle Down" concept during the fear imprint period.

Ideally, your pup should have a corner of its own in each room. And even more ideally, you should be able to direct them to that area when you are, for instance, having guests over, eating dinner, or you simply want them out of the way.

1. Attach your puppy's leash to its collar, grab the leash in your hand, and firmly say **"Settle Down"**, while pointing to the designated area with your other hand.

2. Now, since it will actually need the escort, take it to its spot where there will be a chewy toy waiting for it.

3. Stay there until it lays down and takes the toy.

4. Praise them and immediately give them a treat.

5. Do this in every room in your house, to make sure that your puppy understands that settling down means going to the nearest corner to rest.

Make sure not to leave treats instead of toys in his special spots, as they may mistakenly think that you only want them to eat the treats.

This exercise may take longer if you are dealing with a stubborn pup, but do not lose faith. Just be sure to leave a toy or another object that your pooch really enjoys chewing on, to speed up the process.

#9: Wait (and Okay)

The best way to teach your pup to wait is to use a door for this exercise. It is best to do this with treats and an interior door, but if you live in a house that has a yard, you can also use the front door and the access to outdoors as a reward (or combine it with a yummy treat).

1. Grab a few doggy treats and take your dog with you in the room.

2. Close the door and spend a minute or two with the puppy inside the room. However, do not play games or get them too excited as you need your puppy to be calm for this exercise.

3. Walk to the door, as you usually do. When your puppy comes along, firmly say **"Wait"**.

4. Now, place your hand on the doorknob. Chances are, your pup will start impatiently dancing around and getting between your legs.

5. Open the door, but not more than a crack. If the puppy pushes to go through, say **"No"**, **"Whoops"**, or whatever cue you want to use to let your pup know that it is not supposed to go first.

6. Close the door and go a few steps back. Wait for a moment.

7. When your pup makes eye contact, go to the door again, and say **"Wait"** again. When your puppy moves forward, tell them **"No"** again, and shut the door.

8. Wait for them to get calm. Then, reach for the door again, but only if your pup remains calm. Repeat the process again. If it stays behind you and waits, give them the release command **"Okay"**, and let them step outside.

The point of this exercise is to practice patience and get your puppy to wait when you need them to. To achieve that, you will need to gradually increase the waiting time with each subsequent exercise.

If this doesn't work, you can try luring them with a treat:

1. Grab a treat, go inside a room, and close the door.

2. Crack the door open and say **"Wait"** while holding your treat hand behind your back, so that your puppy stays behind you.

3. Keep your hand there for a couple of seconds, then slowly move it towards the door, while saying **"Okay"**.

4. Let them leave the room, then praise them immediately, and reward them with the treat.

Keep in mind that in order for your pooch to learn the "Wait" command, you will have to be able to do it without luring them with treats. Repeat this exercise for as long as it takes for your puppy to understand what the treat is there for, and then give the previous exercise a try, to practice "Wait" and "Okay" with your puppy without the luring technique.

#10: Excuse Me

"Excuse me" may not be the most basic command, to be honest, but this is the best time to teach your pup to be careful not to get in your way. Because young pups love doing that. As soon as they figure out that blocking your way gets them attention, they start doing it in order to steal some cuddling time from you. They don't care if your arms are full of grocery bags or that you're carrying a heavy laundry basket, and they surely cannot realize that they can trip you up, or even worse, that they can get stepped on.

In order for you to prevent that from happing, a simple verbal cue is used from the 12th week, so that your puppy can learn how to back up politely and respect your space. If you have an older dog, you can practice this exercise with luring treats, but to save yourself some time, as well as to help your puppy understand what it is supposed to do, teaching "Excuse me" to a 12-week-old pup is most effective if done physically:

1. Grab a few treats in your hand and have your puppy stand in front of you.

2. Shuffle your feet underneath their belly, firmly say **"Excuse Me"** and gently move them out of the way.

3. As soon as your puppy is out of your way, praise them with **"Good Boy/Girl"** and give them a treat.

4. Praise them for another minute or so, and then repeat this exercise again. Repeat a

couple of times a day during this growth stage.

Handling and Socializing

This is probably the period during which you will begin taking your puppy outside. It will explore new sights and different places, but it will also be introduced to other living creatures. Do not forget that your pooch loves its two-legged and four-legged friends. Give them access to other puppies, bring them with you when going out for a walk with a friend, and make sure that it meets new faces almost every day. If you cannot do this on your own, ask your puppy's veterinarian to recommend you a puppy class where you can meet other well-managed canines, as well as people so that your puppy can spend some time around them.

Keep in mind that socialization plays a huge part in the puppy's growth and is especially important for the way it will grow to treat people. Frequent socialization doesn't create spoiled dogs, quite the contrary. It just makes them understand that your judgment, when people are concerned, is right, and prevents them from doing something stupid such as barking excessively, being aggressive, or even biting a stranger in the future.

During this period, handling your pup should also be an important part of the schedule. Make sure to regularly touch and check your pup's ears, tail and paws. If your puppy will also be around children, make sure they handle them as well. Your pup needs to get used to connecting with humans, so handling them regularly from the early stages is extremely important.

Teething

12 to 16 weeks is the time when your puppy's teeth will start to shred and fall out, in order for new, permanent teeth to emerge, so do not be surprised if you find white crumbs or rice-sized teeth all over your house.

A puppy's mouth is filled with 28 tiny teeth, and when your puppy is about three or four months old, these razor-sharp teeth will fall out and make room for 42 adult teeth. This period can be extremely painful for the puppy, as their gum will most likely be sore. If you have children, you are probably aware of how uncomfortable a teething baby can be.

Somewhere between the 12th and 16th week, your puppy's teeth will start falling out, and they will become irritated, uncomfortable, and more nervous. Besides offering comfort in the form of petting and spending quality time with them, you should also provide something to ease the pain. Offer quality chew toys and take them to a vet check in order to make sure that everything is progressing the way it should.

16 to 24 Weeks

Welcome to adolescence! This is the stage when you realize that just because your pup knows basic directions doesn't mean that it will be in the mood to respond to them. Some days may be livable, but others may be just too overwhelming. Your puppy will bolt, chase, and nip on pretty much everything mobile. It may bark at you annoyingly when you will not be in the mood to spend the whole afternoon chasing them around, or it may even mount you when it feels like it. At this stage, your pooch will crave attention more than ever. It desires to be the center of it, and good luck to you if you try to take the crown away from them.

Know that all that is perfectly normal. Just like with human adolescence, your puppy is now going through a pretty confusing period that you just have to endure patiently. It needs your guidance now more than ever, so be sure to remind yourself that their outbursts are a normal part of their development and that by not giving up on the training sessions, each day, you are a step closer to having a well-behaved and respectful friend for life.

Once your pooch turns 16 weeks, you should establish a strictly organized training routine that you (and your family members) should control closely. Whatever directions your pup has managed to master can be exercised throughout the whole day. Teaching new directions should be left for the time you've set aside for training your puppy only, as you need to keep them interested and responsive. Otherwise, your puppy may get overwhelmed way too soon, and you will end up investing a lot more effort into the training. Keep the sessions short, but upbeat and positive.

Allowing More Freedom

Even though your pup may seem to be a lot more responsive than 4 weeks ago, it still sees your entire house as a hidden treasure. The urge for digging, chewing, and tearing things apart is still uncontrollable to a great extent. Leaving your pup unattended is just like leaving your teenage son alone in the house for the whole weekend. It's trouble waiting to happen.

You should be able to keep a close eye on your puppy and have them in an enclosed area. When that's not possible, your puppy's free time in the house should still be controlled with a leash.

As your puppy's getting more obedient and the training progresses, you should start allowing more freedom around the house, gradually. Gate a larger area, let them play around unleashed for short periods of time and track their behavior. Don't rush it though. Keep in mind that your puppy is still young and overly excited, so don't think that it has mastered its obedience class ahead of time.

The FIVE Power Words

As soon as your pup learns the ten basic words, you need to start working on enriching its vocabulary. As your puppy is progressing both mentally and physically, you need to teach them five power words that are essential for your pooch's obedience training. Once it is able to master Heel, Stay, No, Come, and Stand-Stay, the afternoon walks in the park will become a real treat for you both.

Heel

Heel means "walk by my side nicely". It means showing your dog that pulling on the leash as you are walking along the street is not acceptable. This is probably the command that most dog owners are impatient for their puppies to master, as there is nothing more rewarding than having your pooch standing and walking calmly by your side. Sure, the heel is not the easiest thing to teach and it may need some time to synchronize, but once your pup gets a handle of it, you will be able to easily maneuver through a crowded park and even call your puppy to heel from a distance.

Introduce

It is recommended to start with the "heel" command inside your home for the first couple of days, as introducing this new command on one of your walks may contribute to diluting the power of the word.

1. Clear out a room and attach your puppy's leash to their collar. Place a few doggy treats inside your pocket.

2. Take the leash and relax your arm straight.

3. Firmly say **"Heel"** and immediately begin walking in a counterclockwise circle, with your puppy on the inside. Make sure to walk in a cheerful and upbeat manner. Keep your head high and keep your shoulders back to give the right message.

4. If your puppy starts walking with you, stop after making a circle by releasing with an **"Ok"**. Praise your

pup immediately and give them a treat.

5. Then, place your pooch in a sitting position and repeat this for four more circles. Do this exercise twice a day.

Work on the Finish

If this sounds too miraculous for your pup's skills, don't worry. You are not the only one. In fact, most pups need quite a bit of training before they manage to learn what "heel" means, so don't despair if your pooch doesn't get it right from the start. Only a handful of pups actually do.

If your puppy is confused and does not get that they should stop when you do, you may need a trick to avoid them pulling on the leash:

Just as you are preparing to stop the circle slow down a bit, and lift your left foot high (just pretend that you are marching) and drop it on the floor very lightly. This action will give your pup a cue that it is supposed to slow down, stop, and end the circle by sitting down by your side.

Change the Pace

Don't be surprised if your pup doesn't (or doesn't want to) understand that you are slowing down. If it is still pulling on the leash, you may need to let them know that you are actually changing the pace:

Start the circle by trotting. Keep your leash hand behind the seam of your pants steady, but relaxed. Lengthen your stride to slow down the pace. Imagine that you are driving a car. Change the gear with a sound such as *Shh or Clk,* to help your pup realize the change.

Try a Different Approach

If the treat reward just doesn't seem to do the trick for your pup here, and it is still unaware of what the" heel" exercise is about, maybe luring them with a treat will help them understand that it is supposed to walk by your side:

1. Attach your puppy's leash to its collar, grab the leash with your left hand, and have a couple of doggy's treats in your right.

2. Keep your right hand by your side, close to their nose.

3. Say **"Heel"** as you start walking in a circle. Just like before, keep them on the inside.

4. If your pooch starts walking by your side, give them one of the treats, but do it on the go – do not stop just yet.

5. After the first circle is over, say **"Heel"** again, and again, give them a treat.

6. Make a few circles, depending on how many treats you are holding in your hand.

7. Release with the word **"Ok"**, stop, and immediately praise your puppy for their behavior.

Practice this command in your home only for now but vary the rooms and directions. Add some distractions gradually, such as having other people in the room, having the TV on, having their favorite toy on the floor, etc. Go between the chairs, around the kitchen island, the coffee table, etc.

The whole point of practicing this exercise in your home is to get the right level of enthusiasm in your voice, as well as to control the pup's position with the luring technique. Once you get rid of the luring treat - which should be done after a week or so after your pup understands the point of the exercise - you should still continue practicing in your home in order to teach your puppy how to flawlessly execute this command, so you can both handle heeling outside the comfort of your home.

Heeling in Public

After a couple of weeks of home training, you are ready to incorporate heel into your walks outside. Don't rush it though. In the beginning, tell your pup to heel after one-fourth of your walk. Keep it small, but increase the heeling distance over the next month, until Buddy has no trouble walking by your side.

Take heeling to another level by practicing it in more crowded situations such as in parking lots.

Keep in mind that in order for this to work, you need to stay calm. If you yell "Heel, heel, heel!", and start jerking your pooch around, it will become confused about the command, get excited to play, and you will only end up diluting the power that the word "Heel" should have. Instead, if it is not quite following you yet, ask yourself whether you are asking too much too soon, and take the exercise back to your backyard. Maybe your pooch simply needs more training before it can successfully handle heeling when strange distractions come his way.

No

In a perfect scenario, you should be able to tell your pup "No" whenever it is doing something that is undesirable, and it is supposed to drop everything without even showing a shred of resistance. It sounds almost miraculous, but you can actually train your pooch to look the other way when you say "No", even if the distraction is too hard to resist.

What Not to Do

In order for you to be able to teach your pup to understand the meaning of the word "No", first you need to understand how to use it properly. There are a couple of mistakes that most people make when teaching the "No" command. To avoid confusing your pooch, make sure NOT TO:

- <u>Shout It</u> – People usually shout the word "No", thinking that they are emphasizing its meaning that way. That is not the truth. By shouting the command, you are only adding fuel to the fire. Shouting to dogs sounds the same as barking to humans. It does not calm down the situation, but adds to the excitement.

- <u>Use It Repetitively</u> – Remember that "No, no, no, no" sounds different than a firm "No". Your pup may not be able to understand the command if you use it repetitively.

- <u>Use It with your puppy's Name</u> – Similarly to using it repetitively, using the command with your puppy's name is also confusing. In fact, most pups think that "No" is actually their second name. If you start using it with their name too often, it may associate this command with something positive (which its name is), and it will clearly have a counter effect.

- <u>Say It After the Action is Over</u> – If you say "No" to your puppy after the action has already been completed, it may not understand what you are upset at them for. Just think about it. Would you understand that I was angry at you for opening the can if I yelled at you after you drank the soda?

Teaching the Concept

Your puppy is still too young to teach them NO outdoors or to do it without the leash. It can be done, sure, but it will require a tremendous amount of effort from your side. The best and easiest way to teach them the NO concept is if you do it indoors, and if your puppy is leashed:

1. Attach the leash to their collar and stay with them in some room in your home.

2. Fill a treat cup and have it with you.

3. Have another family member hide a piece of cheese in another room.

4. Grab their leash and slowly start walking towards the cheese.

5. When they realize the cheese and gets too excited, firmly say **"No"** and immediately shake the treat cup to encourage them to turn their attention to you.

6. Once it is no longer staring at the cheese, but it is interested in what you have in your hand, praise them immediately and give them a single treat.

7. Go back to the other room and repeat the exercise again. The point is for your puppy to get the message that it is not supposed to touch the cheese when it hears you say "No".

Taking It Outside

Once your pup understands what "No" means, you can start incorporating this command into your walks. The best time to instruct this command is when you notice its ear antennas flicker. Firmly say **"No"** and even step away from the distraction in order to emphasize the meaning of the command. Don't forget to praise immediately and reward with a yummy doggy treat for encouragement.

Tip: If you have been using "Ep, ep" with your pup, you don't need to say "No" for minor distractions. Continue training but save this command for more important infractions. To correct when you catch him going astray (such as when sniffing something) just say "Ep, ep" instead.

Stay

When thinking about having a well-behaved puppy, most people are dreaming about mastering the "Stay" command. With the power of this word, you will be able to have your pooch seated for longer periods of time. Having the authority to instruct your puppy to stay when meeting someone, and prevent them from leaving their muddy paws all over that person, will be greatly appreciated.

But don't fool yourself into thinking that you can teach them this direction today and be able to make a ham sandwich in peace tomorrow. Just like with the previous commands, this direction should also be taught progressively.

Here are some rules you need to follow when teaching your pooch to "Stay":

- Do not look directly into your puppy's eyes; this will be too daunting for them. Instead, look over their head.

- When you start out, make sure that you are standing close to them, about 6 inches apart. If you create a longer distance in the beginning, the exercise may come off as scary to your pooch.

- Stand tall at all times. If you bend over, you will send you pooch the message that you're ready to play.

Here is how you can teach your puppy to stay:

1. Put a doggy treat in your puppy's food bowl. Hold the bowl with one of your hands.

2. In order for your pooch to be able to stay in a certain position, you must first instruct him to sit down. So, firmly instruct **"Sit"** while making a stop sign with your hand.

Make sure to hold the hand in front of the puppy's nose.

3. The moment that your puppy sits down, say **"Stay"**.

4. Wait a few seconds to see how your pup will react. If it doesn't move, lower the bowl with treats.

5. Now, chances are, your pooch will disobey and will try to reach the treats. If that happens, take the bowl higher.

6. Repeat again. If it moves, take the bowl even higher. If not, lower it.

7. It's simple; whenever it obeys, lower the bowl. Whenever it misbehaves, you take the bowl higher and it is one step further from getting the treat. The exercise is over when you lower the bowl to the ground and allow them to get the treat. Just remember to praise them verbally when you do that, to let them know that you appreciate their good behavior.

The point of this exercise is to help your pooch understand that staying in place and not moving means getting the treats.

Come

If you ask me, "Come" is probably the trickiest command to teach, and in most cases, puppies cannot understand the true meaning of the word. Why? Because they have either gotten used to associating it with disobedience, or you have managed to poison the cue:

Come as Disobedience – The minute you bring your pup home, you start speaking with him and, believe it or not, teaching him your language. Even if you are not aware of it, your puppy already knows the word "Come", but in his head, it probably doesn't have the same meaning. If you have been chasing your pooch around the house, calling it to come to you desperately, or bribing it with yummy doggy delicacies, be sure that trouble is already brewing. Because your pup probably associates the word "Come" with disobedience or a round of a chasing game.

Come as a Poisoned Cue – If you have used the word "Come" to call out your dog and then did something that they would think of as negative, such as crating them, giving them a bath, or scolding them, that is poisoning the cue. In that case, your pooch is most likely afraid of the word "Come", because in their head, that means that something negative is about to happen.

It is your job to teach them that coming to you is a positive thing. You need to reformat the understanding that your puppy has towards this cue, just keep in mind that you will have to invest some effort, patience, and concentration. Do not expect immediate results, but try to repeat this exercise as often as possible in order to teach them good behavior.

The Right Approach

In order to avoid ending up disappointed, it is important for you to know that you cannot start with this training whenever you feel like it. In order for the lesson to be effective, you need to begin the training just when you are sure that your puppy will actually come when you instruct them to. Otherwise, "Come" will have no meaning. That is why you should train this command, only when your puppy is not preoccupied with other things and when you are sure that you can get their full attention:

1. Go to a clean area that is free of distractions. No TV, no other people, no cats, no toys, nothing.

2. Fill one of your hands with their favorite treats.

3. Make sure to stand a few feet apart from the pup. Let them notice the treat, and as it

begins approaching you, firmly say **"Come"**. It may seem stupid to call your pooch when it is so close to you, but the whole point of this exercise is for them to learn that they should come to you when it hears the word "Come".

4. When your puppy comes to you, open your hand, and let them have their treat. Do not forget to praise verbally.

5. Step away from them again, and repeat the process until you are out of treats.

6. Make sure to increase the distance between you and your pup every day for even more effective training.

Tip: Most dog owners use the word "Come" when trying to bring their puppies inside. Coming in from outdoors is a disappointing and negative thing to puppies. By using this command to get your pooch inside, you may be poisoning the cue. Instead, try to use a different word for this action, such as "Inside".

Stand-Stay

"Stand" is a great command, but just like "Sit", it usually doesn't last for more than a couple of seconds. And while standing up is great for doing a quick paw wipe and avoiding getting mud all over your house, in some situations, you will need your pup to hold that position for a bit longer.

Fortunately, teaching your pooch to remain in a "Stand" position a bit longer is not that difficult. Just follow these next steps:

1. Kneel down in front of them.

2. Place your right hand on the puppy's collar, but make sure that your palm is out.

3. Slide your left hand under their belly.

4. Now, firmly say **"Stand-Stay"** as you gently prop your puppy into a standing position.

5. With your right hand relaxed, slide your left hand onto their thigh.

6. Wait for a couple of seconds and then release with **"Okay".**

7. Increase the pause time gradually. You can start with 2-5 seconds, then try with 8, 12, 15, 20, until your pooch is ready to remain in that position for a full minute.

8. Repeat the previous steps. Once your pooch is standing still, let go. You may need to remind them to **"Stay"** halfway through.

9. Slide your hand from the collar, praise them verbally, and reward them with a yummy treat.

If practiced regularly, puppies don't need much time to catch on. However, if you are bumping into everyday resistance or your pooch is just too stubborn, they may need extra encouragement:

1. Depending on your puppy's height, place a handful of their favorite doggy treats where they can easily sniff them, but cannot reach them.

2. Instruct them to **"Stand-Stay"** in this position. `They will be encouraged to hold that position.

3. Give it a single treat and repeat **"Stand-Stay"** again.

4. Repeat this for as long as there are treats left.

5. After you give it the final treat, release with **"Okay"** and praise them immediately.

6. Increase the length between the treats, and decrease the number of treats, gradually. Ideally, you should be able to have one treat and have them remain that position for about a minute before giving them the reward. After you've managed that, you can start phasing out the reward and practice doing it without being lured.

6 to 9 Months

At this stage, your puppy is going through puberty. This is a pretty confusing time for your pooch, as the two conflicting forces guide their days: 1 – the desire to please you and 2 – the urge to walk his talk.

Communicating with a Pubescent Buddy

Establishing communication with your pubescent puppy is just like trying to talk some sense into your teenage kids – it may seem completely impossible. The most important thing here is to keep your cool, remain calm, and do not let yourself be the one behind the leash. Here are some tips on how to talk to your pooch during this stage:

- Detach – Although this one is not that much of a training technique, but more of a meditation practice that will help you keep your mental calmness, know that being centered can also positively affect your pup, too. Whenever you feel the pressure piling up, breathe in and out to detach yourself from your puppy. Don't take their behavior personally. Just remember that what you are doing will have tremendous results in the end. Be patient.

- Keep the Eye Contact – At this stage, your pooch is confused whether it is the follower or the leader. If you fail to get your puppy to look to you more than you look to him, you are definitely not the leader. If that's the case, reduce the attention you're giving your pooch. Pet them only when it is calm. And remember, always direct its behavior with eye contact.

- Don't Let Them Ignore You – Ignoring is a huge part of growing through puberty, and that is no different for dogs. It is your job, however, to avoid getting ignored by your puppy. If your puppy is on a leash and is challenging you on a direction, you should reinforce your expectation. If it simply ignores you when it is off the leash, withdraw from the situation immediately.

The Hand Signals

The treat is a great way to lure your puppy into cooperating and responding to your directions, as well as to reward the desired behavior. However, if you combine it with a hand signal, you will be able to improve your puppy's ability to focus, which will only contribute to a more successful training session.

Believe it or not, your puppy is able to begin learning hand signals once it is 3 or 4 months old, but I recommend putting an emphasis on this signal once your puppy has learned its directions. Why this period? Because now it is the time when you will most likely bump into resistance and you will need something to intensify your puppy's response.

You should use hand signals in front of their nose to make sure that the attention will be directed to you.

In most cases, the hand signal should be performed by pointing your finger and swinging your right arm from their nose to your face, in order to get your puppy's attention. Once you do that, you can instruct "Sit" or tell him "Okay" when it has been good.

You can also use different signals. For instance, you can flatten your palm in a paddle-like way, flash it in front of their nose and instruct "Stay".

Or you can point your finger and then sweep it from their nose to your eyes to encourage reconnection and get your pooch to "come" to you. If your puppy is far, however, you can get their attention by including a sweeping motion as you instruct them to "Come".

The TOP Directions

If you have been following the exercises from the previous stages regularly, chances are, your puppy already knows most of the commands. You should continue with regular training during this period as well, but now, you will need to extend your control on the directions that are the most familiar to them. Here are some directions that you should use most often:

Walking with "Heel"

You should continue using the "Heel" command to encourage proper walking, however, in this period, you should take your training to a more advanced level. Instead of teaching them in the comfort of your home, take "Heel" outside:

1. Attach the leash to their collar.

2. Let them walk ahead of you.

3. Now, instruct **"Heel"** firmly, and sap your left thigh with your hand.

4. Take a giant step backward gently, to lead your pup back to your side.

5. Once your pup is by your side, instruct the **"Sit"** command, before you release him with a positive **"Ok"**.

6. Make sure to praise immediately and reward with a giant treat for good behavior.

Reinforcing "Sit"

"Sit" is probably one of the first commands that your pup learns, but that doesn't mean that it shouldn't be practiced regularly once it learns how to heel or stand-stay. "Sit" is probably the politest direction, as most believe it to be the human equivalent to please. Make sure to ask your pooch to sit in all situations:

1. When there are distractions around (such as having a new guest over), instruct your pup to **"Sit"**.

2. It will probably just ignore you. (If it doesn't, praise them immediately, and try to practice "Sit" in even more distracting situations).

3. If it ignores you, say **"No"**, and do not give them any attention for some time.

4. Now, try it again, only this time, lure them with a treat. It will probably sit down. Praise and give them the treat.

5. Wait a few minutes before instructing "**Sit**" again, without the treat. If it still doesn't respond, say **"No"** again, place the treat beside you, and do not let them have it.

6. This probably seems easier than it is, but don't lose patience. Practice this exercise for as long as it takes for your pup to learn how to sit on command even with distractions around.

Using "Down" Frequently

"Down" is a direction that can be of great use. Continue to use it often, even in those situations when your puppy doesn't want to cooperate. If that's the case, simply position your pup by gently pressing the pressure point that is between its shoulder blades, while lifting one of its paws to shift the balance. If it starts rolling on the floor or tries to nip your toes, ignore them completely. Many dog trainers say that it helps if you step on the leash when dealing with a naughty dog. That way the dog is only allowed to lie down comfortably, so you can give this a try when faced with one of their tantrums. Release only after they has calmed down.

Try to use "Down" in all kinds of situations. For instance, use it before treating. Instruct them to get down before allowing them to take the treat. Or, use it before dinner. Cover their food bowl with your hand, and instruct them "Down" as you're putting the bowl down.

Taking "No" Outside

Once your puppy learns what "No" means, it is time to take it outside and test if they will still be cooperative even when the wonders of the outdoor world are involved. Practice "No" when the neighbor's cat is around, when there are kids in the park, where your puppy gets distracted by bikers, and is amused by other passing-by temptations.

But, do not try to teach "No" outside when your puppy is unleashed. You may end up chasing them all around the park. Train them to accept "No" when their leash is attached to their collar, and always correct with a sharp and sternest tone.

"Wait" with Distractions

Just like "Sit", this is the period when you have to practice "Wait", but with a lot of distractions involved. Use the same method as with "Sit", try to ignore them if it is being naughty, lure with a treat, try without the treat again, and finally, punish by not allowing them to have the treat, by refusing to give outdoor access, etc. You'd be surprised to learn how well negative reinforcement actually works.

9 to 12 Months

Now that your pup is a teenager, they will begin testing your boundaries, not only to see if it can be cut some slack, but also because it is emotionally more ready and gets more confused by some of your directions. It wonders, perhaps whether instructing the "Down" command when there is only the two of you in the room is different than directing it to lay "Down" when there is company around.

Keep in mind that it is perfectly normal for your pup to be questioning you in this period. If you have been training them from the start and you know that it has managed to learn most of the commands but suddenly shows resistance or takes a bit too long to perform a familiar action, that means that it is questioning your directions.

There is really no other way to get through this period except with patience and persistence. Just remember the two most important things:

1. Decide exactly what you want your pup to do when giving them a direction

2. Always follow through. If your expectations are not crystal clear, how can you expect for your puppy's reaction to be?

If you keep bumping into resistance a bit too often, start using the "No" command more. Alternatively, try the ignoring technique:

1. If your pup is questioning you by not responding to your direction the way they should, stop immediately.

2. If you are at home, go to another room. Do not let your pup see you for a couple of minutes. If you are outside. Stand still and do not move. Take out your phone to check your messages or just look the other way for a minute or two. The point is for you to stop all interactions with them.

3. After ignoring them for a couple of minutes, repeat the given direction again.

4. If it still is not behaving the way it should, ignore them a little bit longer this time. The point is for your puppy to learn that undesired behavior has an undesired outcome, which in this case is you not giving them any attention.

Giving the Clicker a Try

Positive reinforcement is, perhaps, the greatest way for puppies to learn which actions please you and treat them. With the power of the reward, your pup gets encouraged to repeat these actions again in the future, until eventually, they become their normal behavior. But sometimes, even when your pockets are filled with the yummiest doggy treats, the positive training process may progress at a much slower pace than expected. If this happens, do not give up on your pup just yet. There is a trick for you to speed things up a bit and teach them obedience. That trick is called *clicker training.*

Clicker training is a training technique that is combined with or used instead of the normal positive reinforcement routine in order to teach puppies to repeat the behavior that rewards them and avoid those actions that offer no benefit to them. Here, the pup learns that it is the one that controls the outcome, feels more in charge of the training, and is less likely to get overwhelmed by the whole process. Besides being super empowering, clicker training also helps pups look forward to the training sessions, and improve your ability to communicate with your dog.

How Does It Work?

Unlike a normal positive reinforcement training - where you teach your pup a command word - here, you let your pup accidentally stumble upon the desired behavior. For instance, it may perform many "wrong" actions during the day, until it accidentally sits down. Once you see that happening, you give the clicker *a click* and instantly reward your pup. The ultimate goal here is for your pup to associate its action with the click, which it will then associate with the reward, and will get encouraged to repeat that behavior again. To them, the sound of the click equals great things happening.

With clicker training, you use neither commands, physical directions, or any kind of punishment. Here, the process is entirely puppy motivated, and the pup is given the choice to discover what's right and what's wrong, on their own.

Click Equals Treat

In order for you to be able to let your pup learn that a certain behavior is desired, you first need to help them figure out that the sound of the clicker gives them the rewards. Here is how you can make that happen:

1. Fill a shallow dish with some of your pup's favorite doggy treats. Let them sniff you and acknowledge that it is there, but don't let them have any just yet.

2. Sit down on the floor, have the treat dish within your reach, and get comfortable. Grab a treat with one hand and hold the clicker with the other one.

3. Now, *click* the clicker and wait for your pup to come to explore. Chances are, as soon as it hears the sound, their ear antennas will twitch and they will come to investigate where the sound came from.

4. As soon as it comes to you and you see that the *click* has managed to pique its interest, give them a treat. They will probably be confused, not knowing why it is rewarded, but it will also probably not care at first. Just let them enjoy their treat.

5. Repeat this process again. Just remember to always click first, and then treat. Your puppy must learn that the sound of the clicker means that it is getting rewarded.

6. When your pup's attention moves from the clicker to your hand, as soon as it hears the

click, that means that it has already figured out that click equals treat.

7. Once they know what the click signal means, you can use this to point out those actions that you want your pup to repeat. You simply wait for the puppy to perform the desired action first. Once it, puts down its tail to sit, for instance, you immediately click and give them the treat right after it has acknowledged the sound.

8. They may be confused at first, but they will want to understand what made the click sound. And that is the whole point of the clicker training; to allow the puppy to figure things out on their own.

9. Since puppies understand cause-and-effect very well, they will most likely start performing all sorts of different actions in an attempt to hear the click and get the reward. This gives you the opportunity to make a selection of which behavior you want to encourage and also teach your pup which actions it is not getting rewarded for.

Should You Use It?

The clicker is a great way for pups to learn on their own, sure. And it will definitely help them determine which behavior is desired and what actions aren't, there is no doubt about that. However, if you are thinking about replacing the regular positive reinforcement training with the clicker training, you will be making a huge mistake. Why?

The clicker works great if you want to teach your pup a few tricks and show off with your training skills in front of your friends and family. However, when trying to teach obedience, you are in for some disappointment. Since the clicker training doesn't come with command words or other directions that may show the pup the right way, your puppy will never know when the right action is desired.

For instance, if you want your puppy to settle down when you have some guests over and you give the clicker a click, they will not know what is expected of them. Is it to sit down? Play dead? Lift up his paw?

That's why the clicker is not the best option when it comes to teaching discipline. However, you can use the clicker in a combination with your regular positive reinforcement training in order to further encourage your pup to behave better:

1. Simply. choose a command word and follow the steps as instructed in the previous chapter.

2. Before you praise and reward your pup, give the clicker a click. When they acknowledge the sound, say "Good Boy/Girl" and treat as usual.

3. The clicker will help the pup associate the good behavior with the reward and may speed up the training process.

To wrap it up, no, you shouldn't use the clicker as the only obedience training technique, as not receiving clear direction for instilling order can only confuse your bundle of joy. However, if you are dealing with a stubborn pup or your training simply doesn't progress as desired, you can definitely try incorporating the clicker into your regular routine to motivate your puppy to be more cooperative.

Correcting Behavior Problems

You have a puppy. Let's face it, there will be a lot of naughtiness around your house, and that is all normal. Puppies have a lot to learn on their way to becoming adult dogs, and that includes testing your limits and pushing the boundaries to see how far you will actually let them go.

Bad behavior is part of the deal of adopting a puppy. You should be aware that it is in your puppy's nature to show over excitement in ways you find unacceptable. Just like it is a natural thing to be stressed. It is your job to pin-point the reason for the bad behavior, eradicate the culprit, and completely redirect your puppy with nothing but love and understanding.

Correcting behavioral problems requires time and patience, but approaching the issue with an exaggerated reaction can set both you and your puppy to a path that is much harder to come back from.

Shushing the Barker

Having a constant barker in your home is no fun. Being robbed from your good night's sleep is nothing but a headache. But before you try to find a way to shush your barking ball of fur, you first need to determine what makes your pooch bark in the first place. Barking is a dog's way of communicating, and it is how they express themselves. See what your pooch is trying to tell you before you take a step further:

Barking for Attention

Your puppy just has to go through a phase of not being able to bear being alone. It is a normal part of their development. If your puppy is a loud barker when you are preparing to leave the house, here are some tips that may help you solve the problem:

- Do not give them attention. By soothing a protester, you only add fuel to the fire. You will not only make things worse, but you will end up with a spoiled pup.

- Do not leave or enter your house in a grandiose way because they are too exciting for your pup and they're only encouraging the barking even more.

- Grab a hollow bone that is safe for your pup to chew on and fill it with some peanut butter. Offer it to your pup before you leave the house to keep them occupied.

You can also try this:

1. Grab an empty can and put it in your pocket.

2. Get ready to leave the house and stand in the hallway.

3. Chances are, your puppy is already barking their lungs out. Throw the can toward (NOT AT your puppy). The goal here is for them to think that this reaction comes from the environment, not you.

4. When your puppy stops barking, give them attention.

5. Do this for every arrival and departure, until it realizes that stopping means getting the attention.

Barking at Everything

If your puppy is a real barker, then chances are, nothing in your home goes unnoticed. But, living with everlasting barking can be a real pain. If nothing is wrong with them, and you know that it is just an incessant barker, then know that the reason it is doing that is probably because it wants things to go away. For instance, if it barks at a cat, the cat will most likely go away. But if it starts barking at the postman, it may realize that their superpowers aren't as effective. So it will start barking some more and more. And then louder and louder.

If your first thought is to try yelling at them to stop (which is quite understandable given that his barking has become the soundtrack of your life), you will only make things worse. To dogs, yelling is the human way of barking. If you start yelling, they will only think that you are barking too, and that will lead to – that's right – more barking.

There are three things you can do to try to solve this issue:

1. Start (or intensify) training. Your pooch most likely thinks it is the leader and gets ego boosts as he is probably thinking that is his duty to guard the territory. By starting or devoting to a more intense training routine, you will let them know that it is actually you who is in charge of the home and that there are some rules to be followed.

2. Block off lookout posts. If your pup spends a lot of time in front of the window, guarding and keeping eye on things, make sure to block his access. If necessary, crate them more or secure them with a lead that is long enough for them just to lie down comfortably. Increase freedom gradually as

your pooch becomes less interested in barking.

3. Avoid leaving them alone outdoors. If your pooch is confined and unsupervised for longer periods of time, that will only lead to territorial behavior and allow for boredom to swoop in, both of which are usually followed with long and loud periods of barking.

If neither of these seem to do the trick, maybe you can start teaching him new words. Teaching him *Speak* and *Quit* may help you put a stop to their excessive barking:

1. First, you need to teach your pup that *Speak* means *start barking.* To begin this, simulate a visitor. Knock on the door or ring the bell. Make sure that your pocket is filled with doggy treats.

2. The second your pup starts barking say **"Speak"** in a firm tone.

3. Praise and reward them immediately.

4. Do this for a couple of days, until your puppy learns what *speak* means.

5. Once your pup starts barking when you give them the *speak* command, it is time to teach

them to be quiet. Instruct your pup to "**Speak**".

6. Once it starts barking, say **"Quiet"** in a firm tone.

7. Wait for your pup to stop barking. If needed, say **"Quiet"** again.

8. It may take a while for your pup to stop barking, and that's okay. The second it stops, praise them like crazy and give it a treat.

9. Respond for as long as it takes for your pooch to learn that *quiet* means *stop barking.*

Once your pup learns that, you can use this command to shush them whenever their barking starts getting just a bit too much.

Not Accepting Biting

In the first couple of weeks, biting is a normal daily hassle. But while soft mouthing is okay when your pup is playing with you, for some people, it can be a scary, if not a traumatic experience. It is extremely important for you to teach your puppy that their razor-sharp teeth are not made for the human skin while it is still a young pup in order for them to learn right from the start what it cannot play bite with. Not to mention that this may prevent future injuries and even save you from a big fat lawsuit.

This training technique will discourage your pup to bite your skin as a part of its games:

1. Place one of your hands in your pup's mouth and shake it gently until it realizes that you want to play with them.

2. Play with your pup for a while. As long as it is soft-mouthing you and doesn't apply pressure, let them have his fun. The second you feel their teeth piercing a bit sharper, say **"Ouch"** or another negative word, take your hand out, and stop playing with them.

3. Step aside, look away, and do not interact with them for about 30 seconds. Do this for about 5-6 times a day.

4. If your pup doesn't let go of your hand the second you say "Ouch", leave the room immediately and do not let your pup see you for a couple of minutes.

5. When your pup finally realizes that *ouch* means that *it is time to let go of the hand*, you can start teaching them that they

shouldn't play biting with humans under no circumstances.

6. It may take a while for you to get your pup to realize that it shouldn't play biting at all, but you should be patient. To start, simply play with your dog and keep your hand close to its mouth, however, do not place it inside.

7. Wait until your pup starts biting. The second it touches your skin with its teeth, even if it is super gently, say **"Bad Boy/Girl"** or another similar word, get up, and stop interacting with them for a couple of minutes.

8. Do this every time their teeth meet your skin. This way they will eventually learn that biting is unacceptable.

Getting Chewing Under Control

You cannot exactly train your pup not to chew on things, and you should not even try. Chewing is not only a natural instinct and an interesting way to spend their time, but it also contributes to their physical and mental health. By chewing, your pup supports the flow of antibacterial saliva and keeps his gums and teeth stay healthy and strong. That is why appropriate chew toys can jumpstart the healthy development of puppy's permanent teeth and make the whole process a lot less painful.

However, just because it is supposed to chew on things doesn't mean that your new sofa should be all chewed-up. Besides providing rubber toys, appropriate ropes, and marrow bones, there are also some other tricks that can help your pooch keep his teeth away from your possessions:

- Allow plenty of exercise. Most dogs start a chewing contest when they are bored or when they have a fair amount of extra energy that they have to channel somewhere. If you don't want your couch to be that place, make sure to take your puppy on longer walks in order to knock down their urge to chew on things inside the house.

- Use taste deterrents. Taste deterrents are nasty-tasting liquids sold in spray bottles that you can use to discourage the pup from chewing on things. You can find them in most pet stores, and they are pretty cost-effective as your pup will not like the idea of chewing on something that tastes awful. These deterrents usually have no scent at all, so you shouldn't worry about having an unpleasant smell spreading inside your house. Bitter apple is a great choice for a taste deterrent.

When you notice them chewing on something inappropriate, simply grab the spray bottle and spray that object immediately, and let them notice you. After doing so, offer them a safe toy that they can chew on to encourage appropriate behavior.

- Play a "No" and "Good Boy/Girl" game. Lay out several objects on the floor, among which you will place a couple of chew toys. Wait for them to grab an object. If it is an appropriate chewable, say "Good Boy/Girl". If not, say "No" to let your puppy know it should let go of the object.

- Praise them. In many cases, puppies are encouraged to chew on their toys when they are encouraged to do so. Whenever you see them chewing on their toys, praise them to mark the good behavior, and then give them a treat as a reward.

Stopping the Digging Frenzy

If those muddy paws freak you out, relax. You need to learn to accept this behavior as a part of the normal canine instinct. But just because it is natural, it doesn't mean that it is okay for your pup to be passing their time turning your backyard into a construction site. Whether your puppy is fussy, stressed, or just bored, you will need to find a way to make them learn that digging whenever and wherever he feels like it is not acceptable.

Although just like chewing, you cannot exactly train them not to dig. However, there are a few tricks you can do that will discourage this action. The very first thing is to offer a digging spot for your puppy:

1. Pick an area in your backyard that your puppy can use for digging. Make sure to mark the territory so it's easy to distinguish where it's ok to dig and where it's not. If you leave in an apartment, you can provide a sandbox for digging in your bathroom from time to time, or you can even do this with a certain spot in the nearest park.

2. Bring toys to that spot, or even better, bury treats there to encourage your pup to be digging there.

3. Take your pup to that spot on a daily basis and encourage them to dig by instructing her **"Go Dig"** or another command by your choice.

4. When you catch your puppy in the act of digging someplace else, correct with a firm **"No"**.

You can also give some other tricks a try:

- Dogs really dislike the citrus scent. Putting lemon or orange peels in the holes will most likely discourage your pooch from digging there.

- To help your pup learn that digging in certain areas in your yard is not acceptable, you can install some sensors such as sprinkles there.

- Do not spray your pooch with a hose when you catch them in the act. This is a common correction method that many dog owners use, however, this is not only cruel, but it will also make him dig even more if it gets all fussy. Instead, you can try burying some of its own feces. Dogs usually hate the smell and taste of their own feces, so give this a try if nothing else helps.

- Many dogs dig excessively when they are left alone. If that is the case, see if you can leave your pup indoors when leaving the house for a couple of hours.

Discouraging the Jumper

Dogs are social animals. It is in their nature to seek and give attention, as well as to show excitement and lavish us with love when we enter the door. Isn't that one of the main reasons why most people adopt puppies in the first place? Having a small pup jumping up every time he lays eyes on you is cute, but if this behavior is left unchecked, this can easily turn into a 60-pound force trying to knock you over. And that is something that you will begin dreading.

Jumping up is one of those behaviors that dog owners love to hate. Why? Because they usually start as a cute thing that the pup gets rewards for, and then quickly turn into something that can cause an injury to both the dog and the owner. So, what am I trying to say here? Never encourage a pup who is jumping up by rewarding the behavior. And I am not only talking about a reward in the form of a tasty treat. When a pup is jumping up, the reward it is seeking for is your attention. Rob it from that and they will soon stop performing the action that does not elicit the favorable outcome.

Turning Away from the Jump

When your pup jumps, the best response is to simply turn away from it. It may be heartbreaking not to give your pup attention when it is so excited to see you, but this is the most effective way to teach him to control their emotions, and believe me, once it grows into an adult dog, this trick you're teaching them now will be greatly appreciated.

Bring your hands to your chest and avoid eye contact. Once your pup sees that it gets no response, it will soon settle down. Once it is four-on-the-floor, praise them for being calm and reward them with your attention now.

Use Commands

If your pup has already mastered the "Sit" command, you can use this to get it to settle down. Again, as soon as it is on the floor, praise and reward immediately.

Go Out the Door

When you enter your door and you see your pup all excited and jumping up, simply open the door, step aside, and then close the door. Wait for your pup to calm down before going back inside. If your pooch starts jumping up again, repeat this process. Now, this may take a while, but don't lose faith. Your pup will soon pick up that you will not go through unless it greets you in a calm way. Once it does that, praise them like crazy and reward them with your attention. Or a smelly treat. No dog has ever refused that.

Dealing with Separation Anxiety

Puppies hate being left alone. If it is up to them, they will probably follow you to the end of the World. But, they cannot. As much as you both enjoy your time together, there are times when you simply have to leave your pooch alone, and chances are, you have to do it on a daily basis. But just because you hear sad whining when you close the door doesn't mean that your pup is anxious you left them alone. In order for you to be able to help them cope better with separation, you will first need to determine whether it really is anxious or not.

So, what are the signs of separation anxiety in puppies? If your pup is chewing things destructively when left alone, keeps urinating and defecating even if it is house trained, is barking, howling, and whining excessively, develops a habit of excessive digging or keeps scratching the door as an attempt to reunite with you, chances are, your pooch is suffering from separation anxiety.

Do not despair! This is completely normal and it happens in the majority of cases when the dog owner has a full-time job that requires them to leave the house for longer periods of time.

Here are some tips that can help you knock down the anxiety and boost the mood of your pooch a bit while you are away:

- Do not make departures and arrivals a big deal. Keep ignoring your pup while getting ready to leave the house, and then gently pet them on the head before you leave the door. Do not turn to mush with them only to show them your back and close the door. Leaving with kisses and treats will not reassure your pooch. Quite the contrary. That will only leave them stressed out.

- Come up with a "Goodbye" word that you will use every time you leave your home. That will reassure your pup that you will actually get back.

- Make sure to leave the area where the pup will be staying dimly lit, so you can encourage sleep.

- Always leave toys around. Giving your pup something to chew on while alone is a great way for them to keep boredom at bay and not think about being left alone that much.

- If needed, leave the radio on playing relaxing music such as classical music or jazz, if you need to cover unfamiliar sounds and offer reassurance. The best advice is to play that music even when you are together in the house so that your pup will get used to it.

- Spend some time near their crate so that their safe haven will smell like you even after you leave the house. Some owners even leave recently worn pieces of clothes around so that the area will still have a strong scent of you.

- If you come home only to find a mess, do not yell or correct your pup. The correction will not be associated with the destruction that the puppy has caused, but with your arrival. Instead of teaching them to be more disciplined in the future, you are actually contributing to them feeling even more anxious the next time you leave the house. Instead of correcting, try to find a different approach to ensure that the destructive behavior will not happen again.

- If your pup is suffering from severe separation anxiety, consult with your veterinarian. They may suggest you hire a dog walker to take them on long walks, or even for you to sign your puppy up for a doggie daycare.

Keep in mind that separation anxiety is not a result of lack of training. This form of anxiety and obedience have nothing in common, so don't fool yourself into thinking that insufficient training is what causes your pooch to behave destructively when you leave the door. Follow the tips above and see if you can offer reassurance. If you keep providing reassurance from the early stages, your pup will soon learn to accept the routine and you will have no problem to leave your full-grown dog alone when going out in the future. Give it some time and be patient.

Conclusion

Puppies thrive on strictly set routines. If you manage to make the training process a fun and consistent process, your pooch will be encouraged to learn the desired directions in a short period of time.

With the help of this book, you will be able to master all the true-and-tried puppy training techniques and help your puppy grow into an obedient and happy dog that will act respectfully.

Just remember that you are the one leading the way. It is in your puppy's nature to follow, so make sure to show them the right way. The secret formula to obedient puppyhood = patience + persistence. Equip yourself with these qualities and see how strong your owner-dog relationship can really be.

www.ingramcontent.com/pod-product-compliance
Lightning Source LLC
Chambersburg PA
CBHW070043230426
43661CB00005B/730